MAN AND HIS WORLD

D0943144

MAN
AND
HIS WORLD

A MARXIAN VIEW

by

IVAN SVITAK

TRANSLATED BY JARMILA VELTRUSKY

A DELTA BOOK

A DELTA BOOK

Published by
Dell Publishing Co., Inc.
750 Third Avenue,
New York, N. Y. 10017

Copyright © 1970 by Ivan Svitak

Brief portions of this book appeared in
Lidsky smysl kultury by Ivan Svitak,
published in Czechoslovakia,
© Ivan Svitak, 1968

All rights reserved

Delta ® TM 755118, Dell Publishing Co., Inc.
Library of Congress Card Catalog Number: 77-89705
Manufactured in the United States of America
First Delta printing—January 1970

Dedicated to Marxist humanists
who believe in the idea of
socialism with a human face

MAN AND HIS WORLD

Contents

"The Root of Mankind Is Man."

KARL MARX

Introduction

In every closed system of ideas, in every mass ideology or religious faith, there arise new interpretations of the system. These are often regarded as forms of deviation or heresy. Indeed, under certain social circumstances no new form of intellectual dynamics is possible because a closed system of dogmas, and prevailing scientific knowledge blocks *a priori* any other form of consideration concerning human reality. The social conditioning of mass ideologies has been exhaustively investigated by Karl Mannheim and by the more recent exponents of the sociology of knowledge so that it is not controversial theoretically. However, despite theoretical findings, mass political ideologies still have the same irrational and forceful effect and still are controlled by the same principles which lit the stakes of heretics and prepared crusades.

A philosopher in East Europe finds out quickly the truth which has become evident to everybody who has not sacrificed his common sense to the party. He learns that under the conditions of a totalitarian dictatorship, which is a social reality regardless of what the philosopher thinks, he has only two possibilities. He may resign himself to the pseudo-scientific nature of ideological disputes and devote his time, undisturbed, to natural sciences, semantics, logical positivism, Heidegger, or stamp collecting, that is, to any area which ideological problems touch only indirectly. Such a pure scientist can become a university professor or he may make a career for himself in a scientific institute, and, surprisingly, he can cultivate his specialization because he does not disturb the totalitarian dictatorship in any way. The power élite tolerates apolitical scientists as eccentrics whose activities ·it can disregard and upon whom it can even bestow its favor. The élite needs them and they are politically harmless, at least as long as their professional narrow-mindedness does not incite students to the barricades.

The second possibility is far less attractive because it requires from a theoretician, philosopher and every man much more than the safe career of the specialist. Perhaps, it requires something which may be impossible—to change the totalitarian dictatorship, a power monopoly, and the mass ideology through *internal forces of the given society*. Faust, who knows that "alles was entsteht is wert dass es zugrunde geht," must choose the second eventuality, not because he would be unable to master semantic lessons about concepts or a specialized scientific methodology, but because he is attracted by the fundamental, existential problems of our time. However, once a theoretician accepts Sisyphus' burden of the struggle for freedom in the totalitarian dictatorship, he must accept the fact that the method of his struggle is determined *a priori* by the nature of the society—the totalitarian dictatorship, power monopoly, and censorship. He finds himself in a real and at the same time absurd situation in contrast to which an existentialist anxiety is merely an emotional luxury: his mind points out to him the immensity of the task and, on the other hand, his conscience—the elementary human responsibility toward his own freedom and that of others—pushes him into a revolt in which he risks everything and loses everything.

This specifically East European situation of human existence cannot be communicated to people living in another cultural environment in the same way as can the essence of the essays in this book, namely Marxist humanism. Students at Charles University in Prague were quick to grasp the fact that the dynamic core of Marxism is humanism; they learned it even sooner than the censors who banned their writings many times. Students and censors know very well that the *only* practical way to attack dogmatic Stalinism in East Europe is through the humanistic interpretation of Marx. There is no other real politically active possibility in the totalitarian dictatorship. Marxist humanism offers real opposition to Stalinism; it is a true deviation, a heresy punishable in the eyes of the power élite; it is deadly enemy number one which must be eradicated and destroyed if the power élite wants to retain its power. What appears on the surface as an ideological controversy of minor importance about Marx's statements or as a metaphysical dispute about the meaning of socialism is, under East European conditions, the most urgent political question not only for philosophers, but also for students, intelligentsia and workers. This, the most important dimension of the meaning of the essays, may elude the Western reader because he does not understand the full import of ideological disputes which lead to constant persecution by censors, apparatchiks and even serious natural scientists.

Prague in spring 1968 was a surprise only for politicians who did not know that the same critical processes took place within the Czechoslovak society which had engulfed Poland and Hungary in 1956. The peculiar nature of the Czechoslovak circumstances was the relatively high standard of living of an industrially advanced country where it was easy to discourage possible disatisfaction by lowering prices, and where economic difficulties reached the critical point of total bankruptcy only in 1967. Three waves of dissatisfaction among intellectuals—the first following the Twentieth Congress of the Communist party of the Soviet Union in 1956–57, the second in 1963, and the third in 1967—were quelled by repressive measures of the power apparatus without causing more profound changes. The first wave of criticism of Stalinism, in 1956–57, was still entirely in the name of the "cult of personality," and the essay "The Art of Philosophy" reflects this early phase of critical thoughts which emanated from the Philosophy Institute of the Czechoslovak Academy of Sciences in Prague. This criticism was stopped by an administrative act of the apparatus against the institute, by a dismissal of some of its workers, and by a number of censorship measures to silence authors. The second wave, in 1963, was limited to Slovakia and was dissipated much more quickly because at that time the criticism by revisionists was coupled with a more strict repression and a threat of trials. The third wave, in 1967–68, finally had a mass support, and only then was it possible to formulate openly in lectures and articles those problems which in the past could have been published only in the form of a criticism directed against literary and philosophical declarations.

The Soviet occupation confronted us, the Marxist humanists, with a decisive question: What conclusions should we draw from the fact that with our true European interpretation of Marx we stand helpless in front of the Soviet tanks? Is the great idea of a socialist democracy a real alternative and prospect for the countries of the Soviet bloc? Is the attempt for the liberalization of a totalitarian dictatorship a mere illusion which must fail in a critical situation? Does it mean that a movement for wider human freedoms must apply revolutionary methods if its leaders do not want to be defeated? Are these tendencies isolated phenomena of East Europe or do they reflect a general trend in industrial societies in the West as well as the East? The Soviet occupation threw Marxism again into that disrepute in which it existed under Stalin, but it could not destroy the seeds of critical thinking among the people. Marx did not know of totalitarian dictatorship, atomic war, scientific-technological revolution, and the divided world, and he therefore cannot serve as a guide to the empirical politics of today. But Marx understood the necessity of a structural change of the modern industrial society; he understood the basic values of the European humanistic tradition, and in that sense he has not stopped being a source of action. Marx is dead. Long live Marx!

New York, October 28, 1968

The Art
of Philosophy

[1956]

I. *The Philosophy of the Cult of Personality*

It is part of the philosopher's trade always to ask the fundamental question, the question of existence itself; and so, to be logical, we must begin by asking whether philosophy actually exists. If we wished to use Aristotle's expression, we should say that philosophy exists in a state of nonbeing. To put it more clearly, the philosophy we have is not bad; it is nonexistent—at least insofar as we believe that philosophy exists only where there is a real development of abstract theoretical thinking. Philosophy and life are two different things. That truly is so, although the greatest thinkers have held that philosophy is a manifestation of life—a very abstract one, it is true, but nonetheless an expression of the most vital quintessences circulating in the body of society. It is not pleasant to say that today philosophy stands beside life as a cold system of theses. But it is true.

If history were shaped according to a preconceived plan, we could say that its author is a brilliant dramatist. For in the last ten years of the cult of personality he made the most advanced philosophy in the world play a tragedy that has no parallel in the evolution of thought. Philosophy, which in its simplest, traditional definition is the love of wisdom, has now become aversion to thinking; philosophy, which is the fruit of clear, fearless reason, has become a matter of devoted, deeply felt faith; philosophy,

which faced the highest authorities with a coolly critical look in
its eyes, has now stood before the shabbiest platitudes respect-
fully twisting its cap in its hands; philosophy, which demolished
great national traditions in the name of the sovereignty of facts,
has now been violating facts in the name of a petty personal
tradition; philosophy, which was the free flight of creative rap-
ture, has now been creeping on tiptoe, looking back at every
step; philosophy, which lived with its fingers in the wounds of
the age, has now been shutting its eyes to unhealthy symptoms;
philosophy, which placed all its reliance on the laws of history to
guarantee its findings, has now been relying on the fact that its
findings will after all be guaranteed by necessities of a rather
different kind. If the essence of philosophy is wisdom, then
philosophy ceased to exist when it turned into a system of dogmas, based on an emotional bias in favor of socialism.

THE OBSOLESCENCE OF THEORY

Perhaps the most important conclusion to be drawn from the
Twentieth Congress of the Communist party of the Soviet Union
about the causes of the obsolescence of philosophy in recent
times is that theoretical work was cut off from the building of
Communism, that there was a break between theory and practice,
in other words, a violation of one of the basic tenets of Marxism-
Leninism, one of the central principles of scientific theory. This
violation is all the more dangerous in that errors of theory have
immediate practical repercussions and great practical significance.
If we are to correct the mistakes that have been made in this
sector, we must not regard the obsolescence of theory as an abstract deviation from the party line or a misunderstanding of
some theoretical principles, but recognize the social conditions
and causes that brought it about. Anyone who wishes to deal
with a question of this kind must deal with the causes, which lie
outside theory itself. One of Marx's basic ideas is precisely that
even the most abstract forms of social consciousness are determined by social relationships. Though almost everyone, includ-

ing the Pioneers,[1] has now learned the precept that social consciousness is determined by social existence, it requires a truly pioneering spirit to apply this principle when analyzing the present time. While all sorts of people theoretically admit that, in the history of thought, social relationships are constantly being projected into the forms in which we become aware of reality, this principle ceases to apply as soon as we come to the twentieth century. Why is that so?

Marxism always lays stress on the objective side of social evolution, that is, on the conditional character of every social phenomenon even in the present. But when the state of theory itself is examined, this tends to be forgotten. The time has come for us to think more about what it is that objectively conditions theory than to look for mistakes in theory itself. Theory will not pull itself out of the mud by its own bootstraps. In the course of history people have often vainly twisted and turned among problems and circumstances which they took to be given once and for all. The break often came just because they finally called the conditions themselves into question. Unless theory does exactly that, unless it evaluates the conditions which predetermine its own development, it cannot exist except in its textbook form— in its nonbeing.

At present, we have the theory we deserve. That is history's malicious revenge on the theoreticians. In past years, scientific analysis of the conditions of social phenomena was replaced by proofs of loyalty and by the well-known expressions of the cult of personality, while attempts at a more serious analysis were regarded as incorrect and stigmatized as deviations. Theoreticians must now at least make sure that they realize exactly what the situation is, because theory's first step toward regaining consciousness and coming back to life is to become aware of the state it is in. And only if theory rehabilitates itself, will it be able to fulfill its social function again. Out of the whole complicated network of factors that had an unfavorable effect on the development of Marxism-Leninism we can mention only the most important.

[1] Translator's note: Communist-controlled organization for children.

If Marxism is a science, then the principles that apply generally to the relationship of any scientific knowledge to any social institution must apply to it, too. And here the important fact that the laws of science have an objective character holds good; in other words, they are not subject to any arbitrary power. On the contrary, we can accommodate the laws of nature and of society only if we submit ourselves to them. This idea was already expressed by Francis Bacon, and if the old truths of philosophy were held in greater respect, they would no longer appear as brilliant discoveries but as the self-evident truths they are. Since social laws are objective, it follows that the evolution of a given society is first of all governed by the law of social change itself, which always in fact prevails over every institution and its organs, even though at the time people's subjective image of the state of things may be the exact opposite of the true picture. In the era of the cult of personality it was said that the full knowledge of these social laws is vested in the experience of the party, personified in one outstanding individual, or possibly in a group of such individuals. What happened at the Twentieth Congress shows that the central organs' knowledge of these social laws may be incomplete and cannot in any case preclude the possibility of error and mistaken practices.

In what does the leading organs' directing role lie? They provide the impetus, they set the tasks, they correct certain mistakes, they bring out practical questions and problems, they apply laws in practice, they test facts. But their directing role does not lie in direct intervention into the problems of science and philosophy, because science cannot be managed in the way that the economy or relations between classes can. Theory cannot be directed either by commands or by ballot, because it can only be born out of the meeting of opposite points of view and interests; if this does not exist, there is no theory, but only the shadow of its shadow. Hitherto the interpretation of the relationship between theory and direction has been greatly distorted, mainly because of a misunderstanding about the party spirit. It was thought that party spirit meant serving the immediate interests of the party. This view was mainly held by people who had nothing in common with science, not even its basic mark, knowledge; they approached science in the spirit of class-conscious governesses dealing with a naughty child. We are now abandoning this practice forever and beginning to make room for real theoretical work, laying emphasis on the significance of theory as creative work, as the discovery of the new.

So long as the relationship between theory and leadership was interpreted in the old way, theory was, of course, condemned to sterility and turned into apologetics. Theory was never able, or permitted, to move ahead of the official positions, because it was never allowed to be wiser than they. The practice of the labor movement was always given precedence over theory in such a way that theory was condemned to servitude and always repudiated whenever it wished to go beyond the limits of the given practice and in general to begin to be itself. Within the officially prescribed limits, theory was allowed to vegetate, projecting its own limitations into the most abstract spheres; in this shape it became the glorification of limitation and narrow-mindedness, and reaped praises only when its narrow-mindedness had passed all limits. Thus a wrong principle, arising out of certain social forces, entered Marxist theory. The man of action fettered theory at the same moment as the bureaucrat began to feel superior to the people. And so the theory of the society of the future was allowed to exist as theory only on condition that it dealt merely with the society of the past and remained in the nineteenth century, if not still farther back. The significance of any serious work dealing with the theory of the present was extremely limited, because the outcome was known in advance. Theory could either remain silent, which, when it did so, was its most admirable feature in recent years, or fail to remain silent, in which case it was treated with the profound contempt that it thoroughly deserved.

Insofar as it clung to the semblance of life, theory lived in captivity to practice and apologetics. This feature will one day enter the history of Marxist theory as the philosophical equivalent of bureaucratism. At present it is called "dogmatism." That is not correct, because it suggests that it is a matter of the incompetence of individuals and of clinging to precepts, while in fact this clinging is only a certain subjective expression of something far more substantial—the garbling of Marxism, its reshaping in accordance with certain subjective vested interests. The Twentieth Congress permits up to hope that it may now be possible to release theory from its bondage to practice. The importance of theory can be fully appreciated when its importance for the most direct and immediate action is recognized. But dogmatism has, of course, not yet been overcome; on the contrary, it is still holding theory by the throat. Under these circumstances we must not be unduly disturbed if we find that the same people who were yesterday interpreting dialectics on its four principles now go on with Lenin's 16 elements and if they go on putting forward their meta-physical reasoning *about* dialectics as dialectics itself.

The objective laws of social change take precedence over everyone, individuals and institutions alike. *The relationship to these objective laws of the man discovering them is the direct relationship of the theoretician to the object of his discovery*. The laws of this relationship between knowledge and social institutions have absolute validity. But when we are dealing with the relationship between the theory of Marxism-Leninism and the party, these general principles do not go far enough. The concrete manifestation of the general laws is richer; it has its own specific features, its own peculiarities. Marxism-Leninism is itself a scientific instrument for the building of socialist society, it is the theoretical basis of the party, through which Communism is put into practice. Therefore the relationship between them is very close, and this, of course, further increases the possibility that theory will merge into a process of recording and justifying the needs of the moment. Moreover, it must be clearly emphasized that theory does not become scientific by the mere fact that it is used by the central organs of the Communist party. In that case the cult of personality would be scientific theory and not its exact opposite. Whether something does or does not have a theoretical value can be decided only by the *relation of a given theory to reality, to facts*.

The theory of the party is scientific only insofar as it reflects objective laws; whenever it diverges from them, theory in Marxism turns into ideological elements, that is, into elements of a false awareness, of those inevitable illusions, which every period has about itself. Marxism itself, it seems, will develop in a struggle against these aspects. That means that it itself depends on the development of science, which evolves through the conflict of opinions, the clash of different points of view, the overcoming of illusions. *The development of science is a criticism in itself; it cannot be corrected by the exercise of power from without.* Science has always been a system of discoveries, but also of doubts about the conclusions reached. In this sense, doubt and error are part of the development of science. They must not be branded as deviations or stamped with the hallmark of antiparty attitudes. They can be overcome only by means of scientific discussion, not by the intervention of outside powers. What a dim metaphysician the man must be who would eliminate error from the process of learning when, without error, there can be no truth either.

The party requires its theoreticians to popularize the basic findings of Marxism-Leninism and make them widely accessible. That is right. But one of the greatest mistakes of the recent past has been that the function of theory was restricted to this preceptorial service, which means that the distinction between propaganda and science was eliminated. Theory was robbed of its scientific character and its most essential role—to investigate the laws of society. It found itself in a position similar to that of German navigation in former times: just as German navigation reached, in Feuerbach's words, *jusqu'à la mer*, so the freedom of theoretical opinions reached *jusqu'à la vérité*, that is to say, it went as far as truth, but was not allowed out upon it.

THE PHILOSOPHY OF DOGMA

All this is only the gnoseological aspect of modern philosophy. If our thinking is not to be merely platonic, we must take into account the social factors and look for the causes of the defects that we have mentioned. The cult of personality helped dog-matism in that the possibility of developing theory was vested ex-clusively in certain individuals. The fact that thinking and the development of theory is a many-sided social, historical, collective process was overlooked. The cult is one of the causes that led to the stagnation of theory, but it is far from having been the only one and in fact the present tendency to make it a scapegoat for all defects is not entirely justified. It will be necessary to deal with much graver and deeper theoretical problems than the mere cult of personality. The cult will have to be analyzed as a social phenomenon and not as a question of the psychological makeup of a prominent personality. The cult cannot explain everything and to try to make it do so is to exaggerate its real significance. If everything could be solved merely by overcoming this cult, everything would actually have been solved already, while in fact the rejection of the cult merely creates one of the *conditions for the solution of the grave problems that are arising only now when it is being eliminated.*

It is only when we stop regarding the cult as the problem of Stalin personally that we can come to the serious questions, for instance, whether the rejection of the cult goes to the root of the phenomenon that brought the cult into being; in other words, if the forces that stood behind it have been checked. We are only at the beginning of profound changes in socialist society. The Twentieth Congress suggests that at the root of the cult there were certain social forces which drew their strength from the bureaucratic style of work that fettered the people's initiative and restricted the workers' share in political life. The cult is bound up with the grave problem of the role to be played by the state, by the organs of state power and by the social layer which is directly involved in its administration—the bureaucracy. We know that, as a result of the most recent developments, the organs of state power in fact dominated the party. The ending of the class struggle in the USSR, the industrialization of the country, the collectivization and the introduction of a new constitution cre-ated a new political situation and new conditions of life in the

USSR. At that time the organs of internal security were also meant to lose their function inside the country, which they acquired during the civil war and the collectivization, when they were directed against the class enemy. But that did not happen; the organs of internal security retained their functions and in the course of time turned into an instrument that was directed against the people. The functions of internal security grew—further strengthened by the war—into a power that threatened even the soviet administration which it was supposed to be protecting. At that time, too, it proved to be true that *institutions are stronger than people.* Against the background of these social processes— and parallel processes went on in our country—the power of the bureaucracy grew, dominating the enormous state apparatus and silencing any expression of disagreement as an act against the state, long before it could take any theoretical forms. This is how those social forces came into being which had a vested interest in the cult, as much as in the perpetuation of police interference, which was closely connected with the cult.

While this social process was going on, the theoretical precept about the withering away of the state was eliminated and replaced by the opposite conception, that the strengthening of the state is the road to the Communist society of the future. This is a peculiar revival of Lassalle's views about the people's state, which in its fundamental, essential points is totally at variance with Marx and Lenin's conception of the state as an organ of class oppression. The idea that the people are the state, that the interests of both are the same, was simply made up by the bureaucracy which in this sphere, as in philosophy and art, identified itself the more closely—in its own mind and only there— with the people the more alienated from the people it actually became. The empty dogmatism in theory and the dishonest schematism in art were *the fruit of this social situation and not of wrong theories.* The idea of the people's state was used to replace one of the basic tenets of Marxism, that state power must be used to build new social relationships but must then be scrapped in order to give people greater freedom.

The withering away of the state is a complicated social process and it was certainly doubly hard to achieve in the given circumstances, when the country was encircled by capitalism. Nevertheless, though the external, defensive function of the state had to be strengthened, it certainly does not follow that the importance of security organs had to be exaggerated and that the views of the classical writers about the role to be played by the state in the building of socialist relationships in society had to be completely abandoned. The repercussions that these factors had on theoretical and artistic life were very slight compared with the well known events, but they had the same root. Instead of the sphere of artistic creation and theoretical study sharply expanding and the role of the state organs being confined to matters of administration, it was in fact the influence of the state in the sphere of ideological life that expanded; it took over or controlled the function of the scientific and artistic institutions themselves. In this connection we must see its interference in ideological questions in the postwar era in a new light.

What is then at issue, how should we understand the rejection of the cult of personality, what are we to believe?—these are the questions we hear today. The key issue is not the cult; it is the realization that certain new phenomena have arisen in the structure of socialist society. There has come into being a class which has the means to control the whole state apparatus and to dominate all the media that form public opinion. Politically, what is required is the creation of conditions such that this class—which is necessary in any society based on modern industrial production—will be subject to democratic control by the people. Only along these lines can we ensure that the abuses of state power will not occur again, not by merely rejecting the cult of personality. It is not the desire to suppress arbitrary power that will protect us against it, but only the creation of such conditions that the rise of arbitrary power will be impossible. The Twentieth Congress has opened the way, for it has dealt with the question of the political organization of socialist society itself in a new way; that is, it has not seen the organization as something unchangeable and given once and for all. It seems that future developments will enrich the system of the dictatorship of the proletariat by a series of new elements which will enable the people to take much greater initiatives, and especially by certain elements of decentralization in political power. These changes will enable the political system of socialist democracy to surpass in *every* way the political forms created in the nineteenth century in the bourgeois-democratic countries and to enlarge the democratic rights of the people to a degree unheard of in the bourgeois-democratic republics.

Finally, as regards the question "Whom are we to believe?": Today the channels of propaganda are extremely effective and empirical evidence proves how enormous a role they play in forming public opinion. At the same time, modern social life is so complicated that we have to take many events on trust, without being able to check their context. These two circumstances would oblige us to take a very skeptical attitude, if it were not for one comforting fact. In the most fundamental questions, where the immediate experience of working people is involved, it is possible to use sophistry, but outright deception fails. For people cannot be made to believe that black is white and that phenomena in which they themselves participate directly are otherwise than they really are. If the sphere of people's own personal experience is the sphere that is least subject to outside influence, then the question of who is to be believed can best be answered like this: In the first place, we must believe ourselves, our own experience of the life around us. And if we look carefully at the basic questions of life, we shall join the ranks of those who support socialism. The complicated points in the theory of Marxism-Leninism are not there for us to believe but to study and to make up our own minds about. As far as the most difficult questions of the meaning of Marxism-Leninism itself are concerned, we can believe that it is a doctrine which was created in order to emancipate the working class and with it the whole of mankind, that it is a means of winning an ever greater freedom for man and that it contains the most valuable humanist traditions,

those of the brotherhood of nations and of the struggle to liberate
man from exploitation, misery and despotism. The labor movement is strong enough to rid itself of everything that is at variance
with the historical tendencies of the twentieth century.

The whole problem finally comes down to one basic question:
Does the cult of personality *explain* the mistakes of the past or
does the rejection of it only create the conditions for such an
explanation? For either the rejection of the cult will stimulate
a rapid expansion of social theories, or it is a finished result,
which the philosopher is to spend the next four years popular-
izing. *These two conceptions are obviously irreconcilable.* If the
second one is right, there can be no renaissance in philosophy, but
only a change in the manner of arguing. But the congresses of
the Communist parties were not trying to put Lenin in Stalin's
place, but to affirm the authority of facts and scientific conclusions over every other kind of authority. Social phenomena
have their roots in certain social relationships; they are not a
matter of chance or of persons, but a manifestation of some more
general laws.

THE SOCIAL ROLE OF PHILOSOPHY

If we are to be true to ourselves, we must begin these
reflections by considering what role philosophy actually plays,
not what is said about this role when highly placed empiricists
jovially pat the theoretician on the back, mixing in the depths of
their soul one part hypocritical admiration with nine parts sincere
contempt. The social role of philosophy in the period just past
was to act as the handmaid of propaganda. It was generally
thought that the philosopher becomes socially useful only when
he stops being a philosopher. This way of thinking underestimates
the importance of intellectual activity so deeply that it could
not have originated in the head of a worker but only in that
of a half-educated semi-illiterate. Insofar as such opinions are still
held today, it is necessary to say that the philosopher is not
the servant of politicians, the valet of fictitious laws or an ac-

credited clown who pretends to depths of wit and wisdom when he has nothing but a grimace masking an abyss of imbecility. Theory, like the prewar Czech theater, *"services, but is no man's servant."* It is not simply an ornament of politics; its function is to serve life. That is not necessarily the same thing at all, especially when the needs of life and politics clash. Philosophy fulfills its social role only if it lights the way when empiricism is left helpless, if it raises basic questions and answers them, if it turns problems into self-evident truths and if it is capable of looking at self-evident truths as if they were problems—to put it simply, if it thinks and only if it thinks, never otherwise. *The task of philosophy is above all to be intellectually active, to think.* But surely that is obvious? will ask the man who has only just woken from his dogmatic slumber. Of course, it is, but the tragedy is that in the middle of the twentieth century, in the heart of Europe, we must repeat the obvious fact that no society in the world can permanently do without that which has always been and will always be the function of the thinker.

The task of philosophy can also be formulated in general terms as the search for truth. There is greatness in this simplicity—as is so often the case. The philosopher is therefore a man who is seeking truth, who does not have it, but is looking for it. The essence of philosophical thinking lies in this process of seeking, not in finding. Only religious systems claim that they hold the truth, that they have found it. If the philosopher wants to free himself from dogmatism, he must overcome the mentality of the man who owns the truth, who clips the coupons of quotations as he needs them. It is impossible to own truth in this way, just as it is impossible to own the air. Truth is a *res nullius,* something belonging to nobody, precisely because it belongs to everybody who seeks it. Therefore truth is not something that is given; truth is the changing process of life.

People who live in the absolute certainty that they have found the truth are dangerous. They will watch the executions of heretics and criminals, because what they are watching is not an execution and a crime, but an act of justice. Philosophy must enable us to see a crime as a crime, aggression as aggression, imperialism as imperialism, reality as reality. And if it does not do so, it is bad philosophy. The conviction that philosophy can produce a sum of ultimate truths is a religious faith which has nothing to do with science. It is based on the idea that the stage of knowledge that has been reached—for instance, about socialist society—is final, though dialectical materialism's theory of knowledge proves the opposite. This conception of philosophy as a system guaranteed by state power creates several practical problems and difficulties. First of all, it makes the development of theory itself impossible. For example, the key issue of the labor movement and the Marxist parties of the nineteenth century was the strategic orientation toward revolution in the most advanced capitalist countries. The man who was to become the leader of the October Revolution rejected this, first theoretically, then in practice. He rejected the basic thesis, and this had great consequences for theory and even greater for practice, because it changed the whole perspective of the development of the revolutionary movement. Is a long argument necessary to show that such a thing cannot happen today? Every first-year university student would be able to unmask as a Trotskyist-Bukharinist monster the theoretician who ten years ago reached the conclusions that are accepted today. Some foolish people see in this a proof of the strength, unity and loyalty of the Marxist theoreticians. They are cruelly mistaken.

Then there was the problem of orthodoxy and disobedience. Since no scientific controversy properly so called was possible in the theory, but only arguments about the validity of one dogma or another, there was no discussion of the substance of things but only about the validity of precepts. And polemics of this kind generate the need to prevent them from spreading by authoritatively decreeing what is admissible and what is not. That narrows the possibility of free thinking. One cannot help being reminded of the four degrees of theological certainty, in accordance with which a theological handbook will tell you what the theologian can think about freely and how far he can go. Under these circumstances it is inevitable that philosophy devote itself to methods of interpretation appropriate to legal texts rather than engaging in critical analysis. Philosophy plays at being the protector of the purity of art, the guardian of truth. It is not impossible that something is achieved in this way. Even scholasticism with its thisnesses and whatnesses managed to reach a certain depth.

But all these problems arising out of the conception of philosophy as a set of truths constantly clash with critical thinking, with science. In every scientist, and in every scientific discovery, there is a certain amount of skepticism. Skepticism cannot be regarded as a philosophical attitude, because if we are skeptical on principle, we are skeptical also about skepticism and therefore we are not skeptics. But the trait of skepticism, a certain doubt about the scientific conclusion arrived at, is a necessary counterpart of true learning, because it is the source of further progress. If we eliminate skepticism from theoretical research, we shall be left with faith in petrified theses. Moreover, science is a collective process which can come about only through a series of creative acts by scholars. *Science tolerates no authority other than the authority of proof, that is, its own authority*. If that is so, then the free development of science, an open road for the search for truth, is essential. At the same time everything that is based on the prestige of authorities and is not the result of a critical examination and testing of the facts must be barred from science. Where science is not the outcome of a conflict of opinions, there is no science. *Science ends exactly at the point where its freedom ends.* The first act against its freedom always merges into the last act of science *qua* science.

The criticism of past mistakes is necessary, but if we went no further we should not do philosophy a service. Mere rejection leads nowhere, and the modern philosopher cannot teach like the ancient Archesilaos, who affirmed nothing himself but rejected everything. How competent a philosophy is can be seen not in how critical it is of the past but in its ability to look into the future and to provide a positive philosophical program. When

Karl Marx thought about this question a hundred years ago, he felt that philosophers must not come to philosophy with new principles and demand that people fall on their knees before them, but that the fundamental, specific task of philosophy is to reveal the actual laws of social change, to understand what is happening. In this he not only discovered the role of philosophy in the 1840s, but he also enunciated the positive mission of philosophy in *every* society which, *mutatis mutandis*, is still valid today. Our task is nothing less than to understand our own society and the laws of its development; in other words, not to provide new principles of salvation, but to understand where and how the society of the twentieth century is moving, *to master social evolution theoretically*. Let us take the liberty of ignoring the simpletons to whom it is all clear. In the struggle for this understanding of the present time, philosophy cannot become a genuine theoretical discipline unless it is an area for the confrontation of thinkers, not for quarrels between orthodoxy and heresy. Philosophy can be reborn only in this social process and not otherwise.

It would be an illusion to think that new ideas can conquer immediately. After a period which has turned the field of theory into a trampled battlefield full of the corpses of stale formulas and the snares of fictitious profundities, an immediate transformation is not possible. Neither is it necessary. It is enough if these ideas are not silenced or strangled in their cradle. The singularity of the situation lies in the fact that they cannot be suppressed permanently; and if they are not suppressed, they will become irresistible, because they correspond to the social needs of the twentieth century. The laws of history have always been, and will always be, stronger than all the rest. The task of philosophy is to discover these laws in all their complexity and depth, so that theory can fulfill its social role on the road to socialism. That is its mission in life, splendid and heroic, irreplaceable and unsupplantable. We desperately need such a theory, because either we shall have a theory written by the pens of the despised intellectuals or one written by the tracks of tank columns in the soil of Europe.

II. *Some Causes of the Obsolescence of Theory*

In its rational form, dialectics is for a dogmatist, a scandal and an infamy, because in its positive conception of being it includes also the conception of its negation, of its necessary destruction, it conceives every form that arises as being in a state of flux, that is, it sees it in its ephemeral aspect, it does not allow itself to be impressed by anything; it is essentially critical and revolutionary.

—KARL MARX

The present state of social science, especially as regards the socialist societies, is very unsatisfactory. It is interesting to see that the importance of Marx has been recognized in all fields, including musicology and linguistics. But in the science dealing with society, where his significance is radical and central, Marx's contribution has often in fact been rejected. While all sorts of merit has been attributed to Marx and Lenin, and while it has seriously been claimed, for instance, that they created a complete system of esthetics, though that is not true at all, their real contribution—their method of investigating social phenomena—has been pushed into the background. And so it was precisely in the social sciences that the same people who recognized the validity of social laws for the thousands of years of human history turned into vulgar idealists as soon as contemporary problems came into question. While Marxism was being put to sleep, the dust was being brushed off all kinds of traditions, and twentieth-century man was being advised to turn to the classics and, for a contemporary approach, to the films, with their sugary absence of conflict.

How could Marxism have come to be replaced by its opposite, when formally nothing had changed and when the slogans about the purity of theory were constantly repeated? The basic answer probably is that former truths, which reflected a given situation, turned into mere concepts and as such were used to exercise the current situation. It is not the first such case in history. Let us take, for example, the ideology which was subsumed in the nine-teenth century under the political concept of liberalism and which grew out of the French Revolution. The verbal form of the liberal ideals hardly changed at all, and yet what a gulf there lies between the same ideas in the mouth of a revolutionary Jacobin and in the mouth of a nationalist "liberal"! What changed were not the ideas but life itself and the pattern of social relationships. A whole system of ideas may be transformed without its wording changing at all; it is enough if there is a change in its social function and character. The wording can remain untouched and may even be watched over with rabbinical care.

What happened in the recent development of the Marxist method were precisely that the words of Marxism became a shell enclosing the substance of the living work of Marx and Lenin, that is, of ruthlessly critical, revolutionary thinking. Thus a system of precepts became canonized at the moment when the most valuable part—the scientific method of investigating so-ciety—disappeared. So it happened that the dialectics of the social process, its antithetical character, turned into the dialectics of con-cepts. This led directly to the rejection of the idea that internal contradictions are always present in the life of society. The place of real dialectics was taken by the illusion of dialectics and the significant question for theory came to be the relationships between the individual categories and precepts of the system. The vital problems of the conflicts in socialist society were spirited away, off the face of the earth. There arose the charlatanic con-cept of nonantagonistic conflict, which made it possible to tease society without irritating the boss.

As soon as the method lost its meaning and only a system of absolute truths remained, the flow of thought could go on only within the limits of this system, which made the objective ex-pression of the most important conflicts *a priori* impossible. "Officially" life was all smiles and fine weather, while the con-flicts were not recorded. So it was, of course, inevitable that the facts about the objective evolution of society failed to be properly formulated and integrated into a theoretical synthesis and scientific generalization. The flow of thought consisted in an occasional disruption of the filing system caused by the speech of some leading statesman. But the objective evolution of society cannot be stopped and so the changes must be reflected somehow. If the social changes could not be expressed in a scientific form and registered in their objective character and significance, that does not imply that they were not registered at all. They were. They were registered, on the one hand, in the popular form of mass illusions (not only about the cult of personality, but also about the priority of science, tradition, schematism, etc) and, on the other hand, in a pseudo-scientific form, by the *ad hoc* selection of certain precepts to justify the given situation. Hegel and Lenin discovered long ago that the isolation of a single aspect of reality according to the needs of the moment is the very essence of sophistry.

In the intrusion of wrong elements into Marxist theory, much depends on how truth itself is conceived and how far it may be communicated to the people. But if truth is different at different levels of intellectual maturity, there is no reason to protest against the cult of personality, because it is obvious that the highest-placed personality always possesses truth to the highest degree. This way of thinking could not but make us skeptical— but only if we failed to remember that Lenin took the gravest political problems to the people and that he knew only one truth. Lenin did not agree that political twaddle is a substitute for true experience. He knew very well that "at the top as at the bottom there are powerful tendencies that fight against such problems' being truthfully published and honestly evaluated." The idea that there are degrees of truth led to the theoreticians' acceptance of facts in a carefully distilled, hygienic form and drawing their conclusions accordingly. The main point now is to stop this practice. The number of facts that must be kept secret in the interests of the state is insignificant. We must see to it that the raw and undistorted truth appears on the pages of journals and newspapers; it must cease to be the prerogative of status and position and be recognized as every citizen's self-evident right.

As matters stood, the theoretician who tried to solve social problems could not get anywhere, because the only method he could use was the speculative combination of precepts. This method attained a certain state of perfection, especially in philosophy and political economy. It was simply a matter of chance that its technical development did not reach the stage of the *Ars magna combinatoria* of the Scholastic Raymond Lully, who constructed a kind of ideological spinning wheel in which he combined Christian dogmas in such a way that one had only to turn the handle in order to find the truth. Here we should remember the example set by the Mohammedans, who stoned him for it. This method of speculation was futile and worthless and utterly unsuited to any investigation of reality. Most theoreticians coped with this blind alley by plunging into problems of no current relevance, for the same reason that Palacky [2] ended his history with the year 1526, when the Hapsburgs came to power.

What will theory deal with now? What is required is not only a change in the ideological forms in which we perceive reality, but a change in the reality itself. We must not exchange one cult for another, but return to the critical content of the Marxist method; the ideological form of the "return to Lenin" will itself be determined by the dogmatism that had gone before. The central issue in theory is not how to set an intelligent and convincing propaganda against the bad, but how to emancipate theory from the obligation to serve propaganda at all. The emancipation of persons and classes from subjectivism is always the dramatic process of a collision between idealized thinking and science, which is by its very nature hostile to all illusions and always unmasks them.

Therefore theory will not penetrate to the objective, scientific causes of its own state by subjecting its own categories to criticism, but by criticizing the reality which is forcing it into an unscientific position. Theory must rehabilitate itself by fighting its way through to a scientific theory of socialist society and ridding itself of its dogmatic ballast. As soon as this battle is

[2] A leading Czech historian. Ed.

joined, the theoretical fronts to which we have become accustomed in the past will prove to be futile and thinking people will again group themselves not according to their mutual likes and dislikes, or their interest in trifling details, but according to the old question which social change, life itself, will ask with importunate insistence. This question will be put as follows: "Theoretician, artist, do you intend to imbellish the existing conditions with the ornament of your abstractions and to give theory or art an appearance of depth at variance with the truth, or do you intend to make your thinking an instrument for the reshaping of these conditions?" Only along this road can theory win the right to a ruthlessly truthful and entirely untrammeled analysis of socialist society.

Besides the obstacles we have mentioned, the development of theory is also a subject to other circumstances which make the existence of serious theory difficult, if not impossible. There is, for instance, the practice of the publication (or rather non-publication) of state documents. Until the state budget is published in absolute figures and until the basic statistical data are made available, every serious theoretical investigation in the sphere of social science will be extraordinarily difficult, to say the least. The situation leads to some amusing consequences. For example, if a theoretician is to learn any figure from the 1950 census, the minister who is his superior must ask the premier, who then gives instructions, in a personal letter, to the director of the statistical office. Why are these data secret when they are evidence of the sharp growth of socialist society and provide a whole arsenal of arguments for an effective campaign of persuasion? The only way to answer this question is in the words of the ancient Vedic hymn: "Only our dear God knows that, unless even He does not know it."

We should be deceiving ourselves if we imagined that any serious theoretical work dealing with the current problems of socialists society can be done before these obstacles are removed. All that is possible is the semblance of theory, a metaphysical speculation that does not come up to the standards of the Enlightenment, though it may have all the outward attributes of Marxism.

Never in the history of philosophy has the development of a theory been introduced by such poor and unphilosophical prolegomena; but never has it been more necessary to make precisely these points, to indicate the conditions which will determine whether theoretical thinking will be able to develop or not. Theory at present depends on these social and political conditions much more than it is ready to admit, even to itself. What it must do is to turn this dependence to its own profit. Marx said that theory realizes itself in a nation only insofar as it realizes the needs of the nation. Now, too, it will realize itself only insofar as it will convert into reality the development of the people's initiative, the growth of democracy and the expansion of freedom which are so necessary today.

PHILOSOPHY AND IDEOLOGY

So far, the discussion of the current problems of philosophy has not dealt with the gravest problems, which determine the nature of philosophy itself and its role in our society. But it has touched upon them in speaking about the connection between theory and propaganda and about the ideological distortion of Marxism. If philosophy is not yet capable of understanding its social position in the polemical exchange of opinions, it must at least be capable of recognizing the direction in which the revival of theoretical thinking is moving. That is why those who look for the solution in a different direction than they should are doing work of questionable value. Voices are being raised against the most stimulating ideas, which are precisely the ones that can make the greatest contribution to theory.

People who feel strongly about the stagnation of our theory are asking whether philosophy is not turning into ideology. What Marx called ideology was the false awareness that a given class forms of itself, the sphere of subjectivism, illusions and wishes, not of critical science. Lenin used the concept of ideology in a different sense, because, of course, he could not guess that such elements would ever become part of the Marxism itself. It is in the interest of the revival of philosophy to use the old concept, which has acquired a new pertinence. If a philosopher protests against the new use of a concept, what will he do when he sees the whole content of philosophy? But it does no harm if philosophers begin to separate out a little.

In ideology, subjectivism reigns, every man projects his wishes and interests onto the plane of facts, and sees reality not as it is, but as he would like it to be; he substitutes illusion for reality. When he investigates a phenomenon, he does not look for its social causes, but relates it to a social ideal, a personal wish, the opinion of an individual or an authoritative pronouncement instead. So reality is as we want to see it, as we can deduce it from some general precept. For instance, it was generally said that the standard of living in Poland was sharply rising—in accordance with the *a priori* precept that under socialism the standard of living rises—and figures were quoted to prove it. Then we got the opportunity to find out the real value of the zloty and the real situation of the workers. The facts, figures and studies dealing with the question that can be found in old journals are pure ideology, which corresponded to the wishes of the former Polish government, was in apparent agreement with the general precepts about socialism and was useful from a propaganda point of view. But facts cannot go on being violated forever; the conflict between ideological and scientific thinking must become apparent in the end.

Many thinkers before Marx knew how society deceives itself, both intentionally and unintentionally; and Bacon's teaching about idols, and the studies of error made in the Age of Enlightenment brought much that was interesting. But it was left to Marx to show that the ideological distortions of the past and present are not the outcome of an arbitrary subjectivism or voluntarism, of a capricious fancy, but that they consistently reflect the perverse, distorted conditions in which people live. And we do not need to have a high intelligence quotient to realize that thinking along these lines puts us on the track of truth. Because then we stop asking how, when and where some philosopher made up something that did not correspond to the reality, and inquire instead how things really are, if their ideological reflection in art or in theory is a strange, distorted caricature.

How can philosophy get rid of its ideological elements? Among other things, by putting the authority of facts above everything else. For facts have one great advantage—they are objective, they either exist or do not exist, and in that they are philosophical *par excellence*. But as regards the facts of our society, this raw material of science, the philosopher knows very little about them. Some people may think this statement exaggerated, but after all, historical materialists are now beginning to realize that the basic concepts with which they are working are essentially unknown. For instance, the concept of the working class seems straightforward enough, but special centers of research must be set up in order to discover what changes this class has undergone in the last decade. What philosophy needs to start with is a scientific description, embracing all the essential facts of our society, even though its role does not end but only begins here. Those who are already warning us today that we must not cling to mere description are like people who exhort a nonswimmer not to cling to the shallows but to learn to dive off the top springboard.

History has always shown that the development of theory moves from the more abstract conceptions about the laws of a given sphere toward a more concrete and profound knowledge, while an ever-growing mass of empirical material is drawn into the process of learning. In philosophy, too, we must move away from the very general definitions of socialism toward a factual analysis of the specific laws of social change in people's democracies, and not try to exorcise the social reality itself by abstractions drawn from the classics. Both dogmatism in philosophy and schematism in art are manifestations of the loss of concreteness, the failure to understand people's deepest interests, though in one case we have an abstract concept and in the other a tangible picture.

In short, Marxist philosophy, the theory of society, must become a science solidly grounded in facts, which must come before value judgments; it must deal with real things and phenomena, not with unverified ideas and precepts. It must find out before it passes judgment. Learning and judging must go hand in hand, not only for the youngest poet but also for the oldest theoretician of society. We must simply stop working with concepts which we do not know, which were once clear but which in the course of time have changed their meaning. A general description of the current socioeconomic processes is not enough, just as a choice of suitable characters is not enough to make a novel. At present we perceive the social processes of the building of socialism only behind the mask of general laws. In this picturesque carnival of general philosophical categories and subjectivist images of ourselves, we must remove the masks regardless of whether the face we shall discover is beautiful or not. Deprived of the fruits of our wishful thinking, reality may appear poorer, but it will in fact be richer, for reality is always richer than abstraction.

But, of course, the development of philosophy does not depend only on the theoreticians' realizing the need to respect facts, but also on other circumstances, such as the publication of absolute figures about our society, an improvement in the impossible state of our specialized libraries and the swift availability of scientific findings to all. Of course, facts will not create philosophy; the way they are approached and processed is just as important. But nevertheless, if we are to overcome the ideological subjectivist character of present-day philosophy, facts are the basic remedy.

THEORY AND PROPAGANDA

The relationship between theory and propaganda is only one aspect of the relationship between theory and life. It has been said that the demand to relieve theory of its obligation to serve propaganda will mean tearing it away from practice. If we understand the social role of philosophy in its whole relationship to life, we shall see that the emancipation of theory from the shallow propagandism to which it has sunk can only benefit both theory and practice, because under the new conditions philosophy will be able to help practical progaganda much more effectively. In recent years philosophers have been struggling with the problem of how to help propaganda and how to bridge the gap between theory and practice. Philosophy certainly does not refuse to help in the propagation of Marxist ideas, but it does not want that to be its only function. In the past philosophy has devoted itself much more to political propaganda than to its own task—the study of the laws governing politics itself. That must be changed.

Theory and propaganda are two entirely different things, which are related but by no means coincide. Philosophy puts question marks where propaganda puts exclamation marks; philosophy starts from objective observation to which it subordinates its conclusions, propaganda starts from *a priori* premises to which it subordinates objective observation. Propaganda characteristically takes a shortcut between a given fact of daily life and a theoretical conclusion, the philosopher notes the non sequitur in such a conclusion. One thing must be admitted: at any one given moment—but only at that moment—propaganda plays a greater social role than science, it has a greater influence on people. That is why, to the practical politician, it often appears more important than philosophy, which awakens in him the traditional associations with the professor's umbrella, absent-mindedness, poles of dusty books and incomprehensible, eccentric delight in abstractions. Of course, propaganda has many problems in which it needs the help of philosophers, who must not hesitate to give it; but the basic truth remains that the fundamental, philosophical questions must be solved first, and the answers to the other, derivative ones will follow—not vice versa.

We are being warned against intellectuals' dissociating themselves from practice. If one is a Marxist, one rejects such a solution and accepts one's duty to help the labor movement in a purposeful way, without needing any urging to do so. The intelligentsia has always played this role in the ranks of the labor movement. If we look more closely at the intellectuals' dissociation, we must say first of all that the people who criticize the intelligentsia *as a whole,* not distinguishing between those who enrich Marxism through their work and those who put forward wrong views, are not exactly suffering from an excess of intellect themselves. They pragmatically think that science is here to act as an apologist for the existing conditions and that alliance with practice means the defense of their own vested interests. If things appear to be incomprehensible and illogical, and to violate the principles themselves, the philosopher is supposed to help propaganda prove that they are just as they should be. These people do not want an explanation of what happened, but a demonstration that nothing happened. For them, political needs merge into what is immediately useful in day-to-day politics. From their point of view, the books Marx wrote had the least possible contemporary relevance.

There are still other characteristics which sharply distinguish propaganda from theory. Propaganda uses moral arguments, too. But Marxist theory, though it does also evaluate social phenomena morally, does not regard them from so narrow a point of view; it does not become indignant but seeks causes for indignation.

These features of propaganda stem partly from factors that can be eliminated, partly from the nature of propaganda itself, whose primary function is not to explain but to persuade. Some experimental studies in the sociology of public opinion show that the constant repetition of dogmatic and emotionally colored judgments and opinions is incomparably more effective than a scientific, objective analysis and factual argumentation. To put it simply, the nature of science implies certain principles opposite to those of propaganda. To begin with, science is absolutely merciless and ruthless. Like justice, science is impartial, because its knowledge is rooted in reason. The founders of Marxism believed that the more ruthless science is, the better it is for the working class. Marx even wrote that he regards as base any science that accepts orders from outside.

Theory—and especially the theory of society, Marxism—must, of course, be popularized. Propaganda has an important role to play in disseminating the findings of science about our society, about the laws of its development. Nearly all those engaged in social science have an interest in such work and understand the need for it. Philosophy must here especially draw attention to phenomena which day-to-day politics does not, and cannot, tackle. Philosophy must not only defend reality, it must also judge it. That is how it can serve propaganda. The philosophy that discovers problems only when they have ceased to be problems is useless. So we do not want to dissociate philosophy from practice, but from wrong practice, so that we can the more effectively associate it with the struggle of the workers against past mistakes and for socialism.

III. The Transformation of Philosophy

The first condition of philosophy is a free spirit.

—KARL MARX

Philosophers on the whole agree that the consequences of the cult of personality—the scholastic character of the themes, the mania for quotations, the inability to take a creative approach, the decreasing convincingness—have become embedded in theory and that they are the ideological counterpart of certain negative phenomena, especially of the restriction of democracy, the violations of legality and the fettering of the people's initiative. They further agree that it would not help theory if the cult of philosophy replaced the philosophy of the cult and if, from doing odd jobs and taking orders from practice, we somersaulted into the sphere of abstract truths, divorced from their context in time and space. The basic point on which they differ is how radically philosophy must now be transformed in order to overcome its past defects, a question which can be formulated as follows: "Is there to be a revival of Marxist philosophy or an exchange of one dogmatism for another?" In the first case, philosophy must express the new content of recent decades; in the second, no new content is involved, because Stalin's name can simply be left out and all the rest remains as it was.

If we wanted to find a compromise solution, we could say that what we need are such changes as will leave the essence of Marx and Lenin's teaching unaltered. But this kind of thinking has nothing in common with dialectical materialism, because that believes that there are no unchanging essences, that the essence of philosophy, of the social order, of the biological species or of the human personality is precisely *the process of the changes that the phenomenon in question undergoes in time.* The opposite philosophical conception, which presupposes an unchanging essence and the mutability of phenomena, a conception which we meet quite often today in connection with the elucidation of social questions, is pure neo-Kantism; thus, for the second time in the history of Marxism, this is again playing the role of a revisionist ideology. So the basic problem comes down to the confrontation of two contradictory statements. One demands profound changes of content, which will enrich present-day philosophy and thereby also modify its essence; the other insists on the immutable essence of Marxism, which does not change in content and therefore calls only for insignificant modifications. They cannot be reconciled, because, in the second case, the theoretician dealing with social developments cannot go beyond the no-longer-even-quoted quotation and can only put forward new facts to confirm the old precepts. It was not malicious Peitho who threw the apple of discord among the philosophers; it was circumstances themselves.

At the present time a deeper awareness of the historical character of Marxism itself is penetrating Marxist philosophy. This is an extraordinarily valuable idea; for in the past, Marxism was often interpreted quite unhistorically, just as Hegelianism once was. Its transient aspects, which were bound up with certain specific social conditions, and universal laws of history, which are valid under all social conditions, were mixed up together in an unorganic theoretical jumble and the distinction between the particular and the general was lost. In recent times, under the pressure of practical necessity, the idea of the diversity of forms and the specific features of the transition to socialism has prevailed; this is the first time since Lenin that a profound theoretical distinction is made between the transient and the permanent elements in Marxist theory and practice. The philosophical approach which led to this is the approach of creative science, which has nothing in common with the hair-splitting construction of systems or with the triviality of ephemeral journalism. Neither theories nor concepts are immutable, nor are they simply to be scrapped; they are to be surpassed. This means that they transform themselves, retaining their positive content and rejecting what has become obsolete. All the systems of ideas in history have gone through this process, and there is no reason why Marxism should be an exception. So if someone today speaks out about the problems of philosophy, it is not because he wants to destroy the old concepts but to subject thinking itself to this universal law of change. The key issue is whether this critically analytical process, which alone can rid us of dogmatism, will go on, or whether it will be stifled. People may have the best will in the world to free themselves from dogmatism and yet fail to achieve anything. *Only the actual process of intellectual creation and open discussion will rid us of dogmatism.* It is the clash of opinions which is the lethal weapon against dogmatism, and that is why, though it has only just begun, those who are threatened are already raising a great outcry, and why they will do all they can to silence the debate, to intimidate it and suppress it administratively, why they are demanding that the state protect them against adventurism. It would be surprising if things were otherwise, after the 30 years of distortions of Marxism. Decades of dogmatic stagnation cannot be wiped out in a few months. Therefore the philosophers who will take up the task of critically analyzing recent and current developments must wage the battle of ideas without the hope of a swift victory and with the risk of defeat and of administrative intervention. And yet they must perform this task, unless they are ready to sacrifice their reason and to give way before the determined resistance of the old forces of dogmatic revisionism, which are, on the one hand, trying to suppress the discussion and, on the other, proclaiming it to be a war between frogs and mice, since it is not about the role of Herbartism in the Bohemia of the last century. Because theoretical errors cannot be corrected once and for all by a single act, the struggle for the time being is about *the very possibility of differences of opinion*, about the fundamental conditions of philosophy.

Furthermore, social theory must refuse to be satisfied that we know present-day society, and must start from the assumption that we have to learn about it. Somebody once said that in science only one thing is more wonderful than how much we know, and that is how much we do not know. Science must know what it knows but also what it does not know. To show it what it does not know is to show it what its future will be. Social theory must not simply make up hypotheses and norms by logically developing the concept of socialism; *it must discover the characteristics of the real world*. If philosophy once starts out upon this road, which is still often rejected as empiricism or revisionism, it can play its proper role. Otherwise it will not be capable of performing the social function of philosophy but only of apologetics. If we want to defend the ideas which will be great tomorrow, we must abandon those which are ceasing to be great today. *Direct contact with the deepest needs of our life, or the death of thought—that is the alternative facing creation in science and art.* Whoever cannot or will not grasp this is on a sure road to sterile, empty and reactionary traditionalism, which is always intoxicated with the past history of ideas, and always only after they are dead. Every society is an evolving system, subject to the general laws of change, and to grasp the theoretical implications of its new features is an adventure in learning.

The need for philosophical discussion raises one serious question: Should we discuss things which require the disclosure of our own errors? History has seen dozens of situations where progressive people seem to be in agreement with the extreme right, and yet it is a delusion. Between the two seemingly identical points of view there is an absolute abyss. Each has an entirely different content. In a socialist democracy, one is interested in the restoration of the possibility to develop a personal entrepreneurial initiative, that is, of a "democracy" which would somehow make the return to capitalism feasible; the other is trying to create a system of political control by the people, on the basis of the common ownership of the means of production, in such a way as to prevent the repetition of past mistakes and to broaden the freedom of working people.

At present new ideas are sometimes rejected under the pretext that they are politically harmful and they are disposed of by means of some instant political label, such as "intellectual skepticism." As far as the adjective is concerned, there is no need to be ashamed of intellect; after all, Marx and Lenin were intellectuals, too. As regards the skepticism, every science contains some skepticism toward the results it obtains, and it is precisely this skepticism that opens the way to new horizons. There are people who are skeptical about dogmas, and others who are skeptical about the crimes and the reparation of mistakes. What really matters is what the skepticism is directed at. The greatest skeptics, Sextus Empiricus and Michel de Montaigne, won their glorious place in the history of philosophy because they directed their skepticism against dogma. If there is anyone who did not go through a certain amount of skepticism after the Twentieth Congress, he has nothing to be proud of. Such skepticism does not affect the bases of historical materialism; it only destroys the optimism of credulity and illusion.

People who have been, or are now, going through a stage of skepticism about dogmatism are not skeptics. On the contrary, they are the historical optimists of our time because, with nothing behind them but their own shadow and the laws of history, they are joining battle with an opponent who is a thousand times more powerful. If such people really were skeptics, they would keep quiet and watch the developments with the dead eye of a dried cod. "What is truth?" Pilate superciliously asks, and tears his robe to show his indifference to the crime. The supporters of socialist democracy are not skeptics of this kind. They believe that as the foundations of dogmatism crumble, as authorities and traditions fall, the revolutionary substance of Karl Marx's thought, his call for the transformation of what exists and for a new upsurge of people's initiative will come to the fore again. They are sure that Marxism is throwing off its deformations and that scientific philosophy will continue to develop. They are sure that only reason, critical thinking—and no inflamed feelings for socialism, no mysticism of socialist experience—can provide theoretical support for the struggle of the working class; that reason alone, that sole possible organizing power of the human intellect, can rid reality and theory of past mistakes and ensure future progress.

Some people find it terrible and unnatural that, now the cult of personality has been liquidated, each man should be his own authority in theory, and that *recognized* authority has been weakened. But in every form of scientific research the only recognized authority is always that of fact and actually every scientist and scholar is his own authority. This is the natural state of science, of thinking. What is unnatural, on the contrary, is that there are people who do not find it natural, who distinguish between the truth of facts and the truth of the authorities, as if there could be a conflict between them. The dogmatic is a kind of stockholder in ideology; he lives on an income from the classics of Marxism, he clips the coupons of their truths, and so he cannot think otherwise. In the frogs' pools of his brain—as the poet says—everything new looks like a deviation and the very ability to approach problems theoretically seems a defect. So the "philosopher" is always performing a retrospective self-criticism, confessing that in the previous period he was most energetically trying to suppress the ideas which were then new. He finds himself in a state of continual retrospective self-criticism for past mistakes and, at the same time, of continual criticism of the currents which could prevent such mistakes from occurring in the future.

THOUGHT AND THE CULT

The period following the Twentieth Congress of the Soviet Communist party brought many new theoretical problems. The break with dogmatic apologetics, which was the theoretical expression of the cult of personality and a manifestation of re-vision in theory, threw a new light on many facts which had previously been denied. The abolition of the cult of personality was indeed a significant act, but what its significance and social repercussions will be depends on whether it will stimulate the critical work for which the liquidation of the cult marks only the beginning. The abolition of the cult of personality was a precondition of the critical evaluation of the present and the future of socialist society; it is not the result or conclusion of theoretical thinking. So we are not faced with successful solu-tions, which need only to be disseminated, but with *questions which theory could not touch* and which require the best pos-sible intellects. One of these questions is bureaucratism. Whoever solves this sphinx's riddle will be the king of Thebes. But who-ever looks into the sphinx's eyes will turn to stone.

Much is being said about bureaucratism, less written, but theory is silent on the subject. That is not a matter of chance. The bureaucratism that is the legacy of the cult is one of the basic political issues of the present time and it is linked with so many things at once that the solution of this problem is the key to many questions of importance for socialism. If we ask anyone what a bureaucrat is, he will answer that it is his immediate superior. The press portrays the bureaucrat as a disgusting, bald and obese old man who wears black oversleeves and, if possible, adores red tape. This man frantically rubber-stamps everything, treats people with condescension, bears the mark of the rem-nants of capitalism and his wife uses the office car to go to the hairdresser. What a rich, broadly satiric picture to delight the community! What is more, this picture fills a certain social function, because then the reader does not think of looking for the bureaucrat in the handsome, well-built man who is devoted to socialism, has no bald patch or oversleeves and who misuses not his official car but his official power. According to another widespread image, the bureaucrat is a man who spends all his time in the office, who writes memoranda about everything and who is ludicrously pedantic; here bureaucratism is equated with official incompetence. That is why the press feels it necessary to expose the instances of pedantic penny-pinching in the economy of state enterprises, which are proof not of bureaucratism but of simple stupidity, and it does not criticize activities that seriously disrupt the national economy; these have deep roots and do far more damage than the penny-pinching. Finally, there is the general view that bureaucrats must go, goodness knows how. All these are absolutely superficial, unessential aspects of the current brand of bureaucratism.

People have always seen the world in a way directly determined by their social position. Individual exceptions do not invalidate this general law of historical materialism. The bureaucrat looks at the world in his own way. The world is a system of orders and rules, within which the bureaucrat operates. It is not his job to make personal value judgments even about that small part of the world in which his own individual action can make itself felt. He looks at the world through the gap left open between two regulations, and the essence of his activity is to close this gap, because there must be no legal lacunae in a well-run state. He is not interested in the world but only in regulations about the world, not in facts but in the authorities' opinions. The bureaucrat must depersonalize himself as much as possible, so that he can become the instrument of another, superior man or idea. The bureaucrat's view of the world will be lacking in individual, concretely human characteristics, because his social position turns him into a monster of impersonality.

For the bureaucrat, the world revolves through the universe only to permit orders to be carried out, and he projects this conception into his real life. This view of the world, hedged round with authoritative instructions and official positions, has long aroused the interest of writers, but it has been the object of satirists' ridicule rather than of admiring eulogies. The writer and the theoretician have, of course, always been appalled by the state of mind which is natural to the bureaucrat, the state of mind in which a man carries out orders without any critical examination of their content. This creates the most favorable conditions for abuses, because the bureaucrat can never inquire into the merit of the order itself, but only ask what it says. But neither the artist nor the theoretician has ever mistaken a narrow horizon for the end of the world. There is no end of the world. There are only narrow horizons.

Since truth must be sought long and strenuously, it is difficult to decide immediately who is right in unusual and complicated questions. But it is always possible to determine what is bureaucratic thinking and what is not. The wrong tendency is the one which keeps theory in its sterility, which is incapable of explaining social problems in accordance with the true principles of materialism, which is tossing about in logical contradictions and which is obliged to ignore facts, the one which is unproductive and which bypasses the most important problems of present-day life.

If mistakes were made in economics and politics during the transitional period, and if they are now to be corrected, how were these mistakes reflected in the ideological life of science and art? They took the form of distortions of the conceptual content of art and social science, of bureaucratic influences and of the practice of the cult of personality. Bureaucracy is necessary in the sphere of economics and politics, though it must be subject to democratic control; in culture, science and art it has no business at all. What is the relationship of bureaucracy to culture? The wounds that have been inflicted on art and theory make the answer clear enough. The bureaucrats cannot arrest the development of culture, but they can perceptibly maim and cripple it in the most sensitive place, in the conceptual content of what it creates. These tendencies are most evident in the sphere where administrative procedures give bureaucracy the strongest influence, that is, in architecture. Bureaucracy is the enemy of art and theory as such, above all because it seeks to include art and theory in its own preserve of orders and chicanery. But as soon as art and theory allow themselves to be drawn into it they cease to be art and science. They become propaganda which uses certain artistic or scientific media and techniques as its own means of expression. But what kind of art or science is it if it derives its truth from something other than life itself? As soon as art loses touch with reality it is done for, it has committed suicide. It can become nothing but a formal game, formalistic in the worst sense of the word—though it may happen that this very formalism will be praised as an indication of supreme intellectual value. Art, like science, cannot submit to being ordered around by bureaucracy, because they are both essentially free, creative processes and they never have been and never will be anything else.

It is said that bureaucracy is hostile to certain kinds of thinking. That is not true; in fact it is hostile to thinking as such. The bureaucrat cannot stand thinking, because it is a free act while the essence of bureaucracy is its dependence, derivativeness and unfreedom. The only thinking bureaucracy can bear is the dull repetition of the same prescribed idea, but this it goes on repeating with a stupefying persistence. If art and science need the wings of a bird to exist, as leading Marxists have so often said, then the bureaucrat feels that the only way the bird can be allowed to live is in a cage, at best a large cage. The bureaucrat is *a priori* hostile to every thought, because thinking is a creative act and a creative act cannot be prescribed. He cannot bear the process of artistic, scientific or any other creation; it is deeply repugnant to him because it cannot be planned and prescribed, it cannot be controlled by an official document. Creation is the direct relationship of the artist or the theoretician to life and as such it overlooks the bureaucrat and treats him as if he were a nonentity, which is what in the process of creation the bureaucrat really is. Under these circumstances the bureaucrat rears his head to utter the one pathetic and honest cry of which he is capable, a cry that turns him for a moment into Vilem,[3] the despairing romantic, as he cries, "Away, thought!"

If he did no more than that, it would not matter. What is worse is that the bureaucrat decorates the splendid bareness of modern architecture with little columns, dresses statues in swimsuits, takes all the humor out of films and smothers creative thought in quotations. He forces his own poor ideas on science

[3] Translator's note: hero of the poem *Maj* by K. H. Macha.

and art, claiming that they have proved their worth and educational value. In the sphere of culture, bureaucratic interference is simply inadmissible, because the methods of industrial management cannot regulate the life of ideas, but only their interment. It is now generally recognized that administrative interference is always and without exception wrong in the field of religion; so we can hope that this recognition will be extended to other fields of social consciousness which are no less important. Bureaucrats defend themselves by saying that they are fighting liberalism. But the rejection of liberalism can mean only that what artists create and how is not without social significance. But otherwise it must be said that, whatever happens, *laissez faire* must apply in literature, in other words, that *creative freedom*, *unrestricted* by either internal or external censorship, is an axiom of artistic creation. We must be liberal in the sense that every form of artistic expression will have a chance of reaching the public without any bureaucratic alteration and will be exposed only to expert criticism.

The society of the future must be much richer than the society of the past in every respect, and therefore culturally, too. It will bring a diversification of culture and philosophy, not their leveling. Of course, everybody would agree with that. But as soon as we put the question more concretely and speak about censorship and unrestricted freedom to create, many comrades become afraid that they might be defending incorrect opinions and falling under the influence of the remnants of capitalism. This is the confusion due to the ideology of the recent past. Is creative freedom, without restrictions, without quotation marks and with all its implications for the press, really alien to socialism? The unsound tendencies in philosophy and art are those which are incapable of expressing the new content of current events and which accept new ideas only as embellishments of the old. The *crux philosophorum* is always in life itself. Engels once believed that Marxist philosophy must change with every new discovery in natural science. What a hero of dogmatism the man must be who dares to say that "one cannot very well speak about a new content" in Marxist philosophy in relation to the classical writers. Only a bureaucrat in the theory of present-day ideas, and he alone, is incapable of constructing a philosophical equivalent of new phenomena, only he immediately thinks about the strain on his filing system that the new content would represent, only he is capable of throwing insults and accusations of deviation in the face of the most vital currents of our time, only he is getting ready for an administrative intervention at the opportune time.

But this will not make history run backwards. It is impossible to go back, and therefore, however faint the voice that expresses the new features of the present time, it cannot be permanently silenced. That is the most significant element of the current situation, the aspect which makes it possible for Marxist critical thought to be reborn and for the conditions that caused its obsolescence to be understood and changed. Which tendency is philosophy to choose? The old legend says that the great ascetic Simon Stylites spent several decades on top of a pillar, whither he climbed to escape the influence of the sinful world. Only once was he tempted to climb down again, but he overcame the devil's prompting: he stood on one leg. Will critical thinking solve the current problems by standing on one leg, or will it come down from the pillar of dogmatic distortions and petrified simplifications of ideas?

IV. The Necessity of Philosophy

> The philosopher asks what is truth, he does not ask what is currently accepted; he asks what is true for everybody, not what is true for one man. Truths do not know the frontiers of political geography.   —KARL MARX

Philosophical works have a role to play both inside and outside philosophy itself. So we have to judge them as social phenomena and also as expressions of theoretical thinking; and we must bear in mind that Marxist philosophy, which takes the transformation of the world for its motto, strives above all to make theory influence not only thinking but also the historical process itself. This is well-known and there would be no need to stress it if the social context—the connection between theory and objective sociopolitical factors—did not play so important a role, or if it were possible to disregard what is most essential, *the social effect of thought in the given circumstances*. The historian of philosophy who is convinced of the social links between theory and life cannot leave the most essential point—the social function of thought—to the historian of future philosophy, because he is himself the philosopher of future history. That is not a paradox, but the simple consequence of the fact that present-day philosophy includes not only empirical facts but also the unknown content of the future.

Under the present condition, philosophy has two kinds of social function. On the one hand, it is becoming the methodology of the sciences, of logic, cybernetics, in short, of exact science, and so it is ceasing to be philosophy in the traditional sense of the word; on the other hand, it has retained its specific character as a *particular form of consciousness*, distinct from science; it is consciously subjective and begins where science ends. At one of the poles of philosophical thinking there is the logical matrix, the prepared program of the cybernetic organism, at the other, the intimate philosophical diary, the intellectual poetry of everyday human life. Philosophy may have still other kinds of social effect. We cannot defend creative intellectual work in philosophy and elsewhere unless we first accept the fact that philosophy has more than one face and that a philosophy with a considerable element of subjectivity is one of the necessary currents in thinking.

Philosophy is not the lonely meditation of an isolated mind; it is the battlefield of ideas and its content is always critical thought, an interest in truth and not in what a given period accepts as being true. Philosophy seeks the truth and never owns it, never has it; it is always the first light thrown into the darkness, it walks before science and that is why it gropes its way; it is not

a collection of truths but an approach to truth, a process of seeking truth, unfinished, uncompleted, endless, and only so does it
make sense. Therefore philosophers are not people concerned
with ancient concepts; they are critically concerned with the
truth about reality. They do not want to build up concepts into
learned constructions, which look majestic, boasting of the ex-
tensiveness of the compiler's filing system, but which, without
ever having had any real practical significance, become irrevoca-
bly obsolete within a mere 20 years. Against the traditional and
and naïve idea that the philosopher is a learned man who passes
judgment on history we can set the conception of the philosopher
as a thinker who changes the world, a theoretician involved in
shaping history and, through his intellectual activity, closely associated with practice in history, with the real problems of the
people in a given era. Unless the modern philosopher *thinks critically about the need to transform the world and about the real
problems of the present day*, unless he lives through his thinking,
to the test in his own life, his only title to our respect is his gray
hair.

The philosopher can exist only *where the system of values is
open,* because a closed system is antiscientific, it *ipso facto* ex-
cludes vital thinking; so that every critical mind is reduced to
a state where it can do nothing but hew out its own tombstone in
proof of loyalty. Philosophers want to resolve the discord between ideas and reality in favor of reality—by changing it—not
in favor of the abstract systems of ideas. They realize that their
ideas will be judged justly, though unmercifully, by history, but
not by people themselves. Therefore the modern philosopher
wants to understand history and all its laws, so that his ideas can
produce their effect in harmony with the laws that regulate the
evolution of the given society. Only then will theoreticians'
ideas become history's acts of emancipation, only then will they
be in accord with the real essence of science and philosophy, of
critical and free thinking, which is revolutionary under all circumstances. And insofar as the philosopher's life is this kind of
thinking, and thinking is his life, his life's meaning lies precisely

in the development of this critical essence of thought; for otherwise thinking will become a caricature of itself and so die.

It still remains to be said what philosophy is not. Textbooks of philosophy (whether approved by the authorities or not), official philosophical journals, authorized systems, the greater part of the academic output about the standard themes never have been and never will be philosophy. There is only one simple criterion of what is and what is not philosophy: does it make you think, does it raise questions, does it make you cudgel your brains? So it is philosophy which, in whatever form it may be—novel, essay, scientific treatise, mathematical formula, poem—turns a man into a *questioner*, that is, into a philosopher. From the time of his childhood man humanizes himself by inquiring, by persistently asking questions, and philosophy reminds him of his forgotten childhood ability to see problems behind apparent certainties. Philosophy does not leave the reader in mental peace, in intellectual detachment and in the weary boredom that is exuded by the books with which the student of philosophy is obliged to deaden his mind until his creative impotence reaches the point where it is certified by a degree in philosophy.

THE FATE OF THE CRITICAL SPIRIT

The cult of personality suppressed the critical spirit, and the critic himself, in a way which not critics but history itself will criticize. The discussion which at one time appeared in the pages of the *Literarni Noviny* reflected the effort to break out of the long-standing philosophical stagnation. Even though the discussion had many weak points, yet it should now, after this lapse of time, be judged not only by the standards of apologists and petty bureaucrats but also by those of history. The Marxist philosopher who is not concerned with the thoretical consistency of his speculations but with the transformation of the world must be competent enough to anticipate the social effects of the ideas which he is propagating. Otherwise his theory is not only impractical but also wrong. Whatever merit the views expressed in the discussion may have had in themselves, they were refuted by something much more trenchant than the analysis of their logical and theoretical errors, by the actual practice of society and life itself. Starting from this point, we must recognize, now that we have the benefit of hindsight, that the critics were moving in a somewhat different direction than the main current of events in the historical evolution in the Czechoslovak Republic in 1956. *Was this the fault of those who took part in the discussion*, or are there historical forces at play that invariably prevail over mere verbal arguments? The critical spirit is not the same thing as the usual critical apparatus. This always makes it possible, with the use of excerpts and quotations, to fill a third of each page with footnotes, even in a completely sterile spirit. Surely criticism is not a matter of references and quotations but of a man's attitude to reality. To use Voltaire's turn of phrase, the criticism that tears the doves to pieces and leaves the vultures in peace is worthless.

Philosophy is the same thing as critical thinking and to say about someone that he lacks the critical element is to deny him the character of a philosopher. The critical spirit, the essence of philosophy, has always been the only thing that the philosopher must never give up. He may lose everything, give away everything or sacrifice everything: influence, power, prosperity, peace of mind, contentedness, happiness, money, friends, love. He has lost nothing if he keeps his inalienable personal possession—his courage, his critical spirit. The unfavorable reaction to the views about ideology or Hegel that were put forward at the time cannot be explained apart from the question of *why* the treatment of these narrow problems in the articles of unknown people suddenly provoked so much interest. The authors did not want to put obstacles in the way of socialism; the discussion was an expression of the upsurge of vitality in political life in 1956 which, by the dialectics of history itself, was perverted to ends which had never been intended, as happened to several of the pronouncements of the Twentieth Congress. The impression that the philosophers were aiming at some petty-bourgeois, revisionist or anti-social goals is an illusion due to the mixing together of various, qualitatively different social trends called forth by the Twentieth Congress. It is further the result of a shortcut from philosophy to politics and from discussion to petty-bourgeois moods; meanwhile we are quite simply ignoring the most essential point: *the context of the problems raised at the Twentieth Congress and of their repercussions.*

What then was the discussion in 1956 all about? The issue was not an antiparty platform or a hidden opposition, but an abortive effort to put the conclusions of the Twentieth Congress into effect, an attempt which was made not only in good faith but also with enthusiasm for the perspectives opened by the Congress. That is just as stubborn a fact as the other fact, unfavorable to the discussion, that in the conditions of the time—which are not, of course, of the philosophers' making but the result of historical circumstances—this tendency was not successful insofar as its development went beyond the framework of philosophy. From a strictly philosophical point of view the discussion represented an attempt to overcome dogmatic attitudes; it brought new opinions and also some mistaken ones, which were corrected in the course of the discussion. The stir created by obviously exaggerated opinions could have been avoided if some comrades had not read newspaper articles with colored pencils in hand, as if they were the works of Kant. The discussion as a whole had its positive side, and if it had not subsequently become necessary to find some representatives of philosophical revisionism here, nobody could have attributed to these articles an almost central significance for the evaluation of our philosophy. They were never that important. They were not manifestoes but current popular essays about the philosophical problems of our time. Of course, as soon as we begin to judge them differently and to seek in them an integrated system of theses with a political purpose, the facts look different; but that is only due to the judge's distorted point of view, which projects into the articles something that was never there. The importance of the discussion is then exaggerated and the proportion of the mistakes made in the course of it is magnified.

It is important to get a true picture of the discussion in all its aspects, because nowadays, when people approach philosophical debate, they are no longer concerned only with the factual correctness or incorrectness of any given opinions, but with the principle of discussion itself and with the conditions of future work in philosophy. If philosophy is to develop as a science, then the outcome of the first serious philosophical discussion in the last ten years must not be simple rejection; we must surely try at least to go beyond the opinions then expressed, so that we can judge both sides in the discussion in all fairness. This is vital to the further evolution of philosophy. Unless a discussion of the fundamental points is possible, unless views that have not first been approved by internal censorship can meet and clash, there can be no real philosophy but only the shadow of a shadow, only a dull chewing of the cud by minds locked up in their stable of expediency. Philosophers can produce all sorts of things under such conditions, but they will not understand the real relationships between facts, because they have made such an understanding impossible in advance. They are shut in the shell of their stagnation; they are not an incarnation of living thought but the philosophers of their own nonexistence. They simply go on piling up already familiar ideas, endlessly repeating the same things, so that they finally arrive at the "foolish infinity" they long for without having learned anything. They keep going round in the vicious circle of their certainties, which they have not even verified for themselves, because the verification of an opinion presupposes at least a temporary skepticism about its correctness. But it is not the philosopher alone who decides whether he will be a white-collar worker looking after his index cards and keeping out of trouble or simply a thinker; that depends also on the conditions under which he can become a thinker, the intellectual climate of the society in which he lives.

If philosophy is to develop as a science, then its errors, too, must be recognized as a natural part of the road to the truth we are seeking. They must be overcome, certainly, but simply as errors and not as acts against the state or as political deviations. In solving philosophical problems we must retain the specific features of this form of social consciousness, which is analogous to the resolution of contradictions in science. The area in which the scientist lives should not—so far as possible—be disturbed by attitudes alien to science. The contradictions are to be solved within the domain of science. That has been an accepted axiom of scientific research since classical Greece; it is simply what the freedom of science means. Marxism is its fulfillment, confirmation and extension. Maybe I do not rightly understand what we are being told about the party spirit of philosophy, a problem which did not come up until the period of dogmatism, but I know for a fact that the work of Marx and Lenin is a result of free inquiry, that it was their very freedom which gave them their party spirit. It is not true that the specific features of Marxist philosophy, which is the world view of the Communist party, supersede the very foundations of scientific inquiry. *The axiom that people must seek truth freely, without external pressure, has always been and will remain the backbone of science—and of scientists, too.*

The forcible introduction of ideological elements discredited the very idea of philosophical discussion, because the scholar who is not a philosopher immediately thinks of the discussion in history which led to the liquidation of the school of Pokrovsky,[4] the discussion in philosophy which led to the liquidation of the Deborin [4] school of thought, the discussion which led to the liquidation of the Pashukanis [4] school in law, the discussions about art which led to poets' suicides and to the progressive liquidation of the avant-garde, the discussion about biology which was the funeral of genetics, the philosophical attacks on modern logic, cybernetics, physics, etc. Thus philosophy distorted the drive of the Marxist conception of the world to develop itself by assimilating specific scientific disciplines and, during the cult of personality, became so firmly enclosed a doctrine that *it must now first open itself out both to the sciences and to other philosophies before it can fulfill its social function.* It must put aside its dogmatic quarrelsomeness and acquire a spirit of scientific tolerance;

[4] Leading Soviet scientists in the 1920s. Ed.

it must put aside its normative postulates and come closer to objectively empirical reality; in short, it must *rehabilitate itself as discipline*, which may transcend science but which never falls below the level of free intellectual creation. The institutional bureaucratic ideology is incapable of such a transformation and we should quietly let it die in the indifferent backwaters of academicism if the "dead were not pursuing the living," or rather if the dead were not trying to bring themselves back to life by putting the living to death. But the outcome is settled in advance. The romantic Promethean vision of the free man liberating himself from the gods, from the forces of alienation and from his own dehumanization, this quintessence of European thinking which gave birth to the work of Karl Marx, is coming true just as irresistibly now as in the myth of the liberation of Prometheus. Zeus may chain the bearer of the idea of revolt to the rocks of the Caucasus and have his liver daily torn out and consumed by a vulture, but he cannot resist the forces foretold by the prophecy which as an inexorable fate, free the rebel god and deprive Zeus of power.

THE PERSPECTIVES OF PHILOSOPHY

People find it natural today to think about what society should look like 20 years from now. Scientists calculate economic trends for a hundred years ahead, and the fact that people are the agents of enormous social changes is a part of the modern man's everyday consciousness. The transformation of the world and the permanence of change no longer surprise anyone; nor do the extraordinary consequences of the application of these phenomena to the old forms of thought, to social relationships and to the human condition. So philosophy, too, as a view of the world derived from this transformation of the world and from the trend of evolution is subject to radical change and raises a number of questions. Let us try to formulate them and to suggest the possible lines along which they could be answered, revealing hypothetical changes in the evolution of philosophical thinking.

Will philosophy exist at all in the future? It is generally recognized today that in the course of history the subject of philosophy has changed even within one single social order, in other words, that the subject of philosophy is susceptible to changes in time. And the historical character of philosophy can also be seen in the fact that philosophy as a specific form of consciousness is itself subject to the laws of change. In this conception, the traditional clash between philosophical idealism and materialism turns into a clash between scientific and unscientific conceptions, and philosophy falls back among the retreating forms of social consciousness. It is said that these forms of social consciousness will take over the classical problems of philosophy. The tendency to give philosophical problems a scientific form, to quantify qualitative phenomena and to introduce these techniques into the sphere of social science cannot do away with the simple truth that man does not form his views about the world on the basis of the findings of science and of the concrete representations of art; that what has always been, and will always remain, decisive for him is his own experience of life; and it is this, in confrontation with the objectivity of science and the subjectivity of artistic expression, that over and over again creates the need for a world view, a philosophy. It is just as likely that the importance of philosophical material in relation to the role of science will decline as it is unlikely that the philosophical problems of man's opinions about himself, the world, society and the place of the human race in the universe will disappear.

If philosophy goes on existing as a special form of social consciousness which cannot be reduced to science and art, can we expect further development to bring new philosophies? We can formulate the question more precisely: Will the history of future philosophy be continuous or discontinuous with the present tendencies? As soon as we accept the idea of the historical character of the subject matter of philosophy, then it is more likely that in the continuing process of the differentiation of its subject matter the evolution will be discontinuous with the present trends. We can foresee in particular that an end will be put to the present-day tendency to break up philosophy into ontology, gnoseology and anthropology, which used to assert their claims to wholeness though they always reduced either man to a perceptive being or the world to a world of essences or else again man to a unique form of existence. Meanwhile there is a clear trend in world philosophy which suggests that anthropology, which has the support of several basic realities, will be victorious in the conflict between the ontological and the gnoseological orientations. Science is swallowing up steadily growing sectors of classical ontology and gnoseology and making the traditional problems of the relationship between subject and object or the concept of matter more and more exact; the anthropological branch is least affected by this process, if for no other reason than that man's personality cannot be swallowed up by science, it is unique. Science can operate with unique phenomena only when it subjects them to general laws, that is, when it removes their uniqueness and emphasizes their universality. It can demonstrate the various kinds of dependence to which man is subject as a social being, but insofar as man is conceived as a unique, unrepeatable and for that very reason valuable personality—which is the tradition of antiquity, Christianity and humanism of Europe in contrast to other cultures—then science, to describe man exhaustively, would have to reduce him to a particular variety of machine and deprive him of his subjective reality. Man is not only the sum of his social relationships; he is also the sum of a unique experience of life; man is a phenomenon with no analogy. The permanent validity of philosophical problems derives from this specific aspect of the human species, and this also suggests that the anthropological elements in philosophy will grow.

How will the future philosophies be created? This is really a question about the changes that accompanied the rise of qualitatively new systems inside the immanent development of philosophical material. The history of philosophy shows that the basic processes which predetermine the shape of future philosophy take the form of discoveries of new antinomies, of the growth of certain contradictory points of view, of an antithetical development. At the same time we can always notice at least five basic processes, which may also hold good for the future: (1) the process of shaping an ideology of a higher social order (and a wider cultural compass), transforming the lower ideology (without destroying it); (2) the process of changes in the image of the world and the conception of the world which is subject to qualitative changes ensuing from the transformations of society; (3) the process of the structural changes in the mutual relationships and conditions of individual forms of social consciousness; (4) the process of changes in the conception of man and in the ideas about the value, meaning and goal of his existence; (5) the process of structural changes inside philosophy itself, changes in the relationships between its disciplines. If we accept the view that certain mutations in the consciousness of the human race have been brought about by the transformations of the economic structures of previous societies, we cannot affirm that the same thing will not happen in the future. At the same time there is certainly still no agreement whether we shall come first to a series of local polycentric ideologies or to an ideology of the whole unified world, whether the image of the world will be derived from the pattern of present tendencies, to what extent the growing field of scientific knowledge will change the structural relationships between social and individual consciousness, whether philosophical immanence will go on oscillating between objectivity and subjectivity, which aspects of human existence will be emphasized in the future conception of man.

What will be the role of future philosophy in society? What will its functions be? Just as the foregoing question of the immanent evolution of philosophy can be answered by projecting the existing trends into the future, so in the question about its social roots we can fruitfully consult history. So far every philosophical system has always developed at least four main social functions: (1) It was created as the personal experience of life of a man who expressed the consciousness, the conceptions and the social feeling of his time in a single generalized form; (2) in a popularized, often distorted and perverted shape it served as a mass ideology, proposing certain values as binding norms; (3) it performed the function of a knowledge of the world, of society and of man, with various degrees of accuracy and faithfulness; (4) it was an instrument for interpreting the world and giving people their concrete orientation in life. These social functions will also be included in the philosophy of tomorrow, which might be able to reconcile the scientific cognitive aspect with mass ideology and the personal experience of man. This form of future philosophy would correspond to the growing complexity in the pattern of all forms of social consciousness. The isolated aspects that we have known hitherto (mass ideology, the methods of scientific inquiry, personal experience of the world, the normative view of the world) have a tendency to unite, to synthesize. Philosophy is now an instrument for learning about and changing the world, an instrument of man's personal orientation, a method of scientific inquiry, a class weapon, the theoretical basis for state politics. Whatever the synthesis will be, it is still very probable that it will be the infinitive universe of man's personality, into which the thinker will send out his anthroponautic research satellites.

Who will be engaged in this philosophy, how and why? Universities, institutional organs, institutes? State-approved professors, licensed experts, supervised officials in philosophical institutes? Will the means and methods of the pursuit of knowledge come rather to resemble the methodology of exact science, the techniques of art or the contemplation of essences? The people who will be productively engaged in philosophy will be those who, whatever their professional occupation may be, are preoccupied by the question of what their own life means and who seek in philosophy their own meaning, the meaning of man. As the form of the basic questions of philosophy has kept changing in the course of time and constantly taking on a new time coloration, so the final cause of philosophical creation, Job's struggle with the meaning of the existence of society and of man as an individual personality, remained unchanged. The significance of philosophy could oscillate between parasitic ideology and the useless art of logical thought, between the excess of problems and such points as are best left to experts, between the meaningless fossils of bygone circumstances and the most urgent and world-shaping doctrine. The fundamental questions of philosophy may one day be reformulated in an unrecognizable form, the current problems will sink into profound insignificance and futility, perhaps even the wellsprings of philosophical creation will change and, after the reign of reason, methods of objectivizing the individual and emotional experience of man will be found. But it is not likely that the usefulness of the love of wisdom—which is the only true definition of philosophy—will be shaken. On the contrary, now that the special domains of knowledge about nature and then about society have broken away from philosophy, the field remains open for the dialectics of man.

What will be the place of philosophy in human life? While man was a hominized being, he had a view of the world, but of course it was never philosophical (still less scientific); and he built up this view of his out of various theoretical and practical sources, his personal experience, his common sense, his speculative metaphysical reflection, his religious faith, his subjective, incommunicable experience, out of the data of science. The world view has played, and probably will go on playing, in human life the role of a personal philosophy, of the poetry of thought, of the theory of one's own life; it will be the growing consciousness of the way man leads his life in practice, an omnipresent philosophy of human existence and the doctrine of man's own liberation from the forms of ever-possible alienation. That is one, intimate aspect of future science. The other will, on the contrary, be strikingly social, because philosophy will have to do more to ensure the cooperation between men that is called for by the growing complexity of technology. Philosophy as the sphere of values will have a much greater directing influence on the future of humanity; it will guarantee man's future, and that will be its main social function. So philosophy will go on dealing with the deepest questions of man's life, or it will be useless. It will go on strengthening unique man's inner resistance to the depersonalizing forces of modern technology and of the social relationships of industrial societies, it will derive from independent thinking and it will itself be independent thought, or it will pretend to social functions which it does not have and with which it cannot cope. "Philosophy must remind every man that *he can be himself* and that he ceases to be man when he surrenders this privilege" (Jaspers).

The philosophy of the future will not be a closed system but an open inquiry and nobody will ever take away from it those questions which follow from the very existence of man. People are obliged to solve the questions of their own meaning, not because they are under the influence of some ridiculous obsession, as when a psychopath asks why he has two hands rather than three, but because they must always solve the ageless problems afresh and in a different way. People ask questions about the meaning of history and of the world and endeavor to find the answers. The fact that it is man who shapes the meaning by his own decision distinguishes *Homo sapiens* from animals. Speculative self-will, which is often confused with philosophy, will, of course, go on generating illusions and deceptions in the human mind, perhaps in order to invite the human intellect to take part in the dialectics of the construction and destruction of ideological systems. Bad philosophy will go on taking only fictitious possession of the world, just as the murderer possesses the corpse, if people allow the fate of man in his uniqueness to bow before the glorification of the personality, the mechanism of impersonal forces or the apologetics of power. The negations of philosophy are undoubtedly necessary, just as its humanist mission, its own necessity, is. The wisdom of the Far East says that we make the path only after having trodden it in the earth, by walking along it. Philosophy has before it an open horizon of questions and an untrodden path to its future.

Anthropological Conditions
of Modern Culture

[1964]

> Art is not truth, art is a lie which teaches us to understand truth.
> —PABLO PICASSO

In our magnificent and cruel century, so boyishly enthralled with technology, there is developing, in the midst of the computers, the guided missiles and the bleeding of cosmic hardware, a rationalist attitude, founded on experience, which reaches its intellectual apogee in the scientific conception of the universe. If, in assessing the role of art in this society, fascinated as it is by the mechanics of the inhuman, we were to take into account only the sharply growing tendency to interpret all reality in scientific terms, we should see ahead of us a somber prospect, a vision of man gradually becoming a dull rationalist, completely in control of his feelings, but deprived of his emotions and fantasy, like some kind of eunuch, and at the same time becoming a willing cog in the machine of an almighty state. In this perspective, man would be deprived of the freedom to choose to be himself and would thus turn into a kind of anti-man.

But it would be wrong to take this pessimistic view, because at the very core of human life there lies another source of spiritual activity—the power of the imagination, of creative fantasy—the eternal source of art. Man's spiritual activity exists only in the permanent tension of its antinomies, in the antithetical unity of the scientific approach and fantasy, imagination and rationality, reason and emotion, absurdity and common sense. Therefore, in-spite of all the trends that try to embalm the past by all the means of power, influence and state prizes at their disposal, man's personality possesses, by its very essence, this invincible strength on which art not only constantly draws, but from which it must always start if it is to remain art and to maintain its specific social role.

Art has never been mere imitation, simple mimesis; it has always implied a whole view of the world and carried a religious, philosophical, mythical or scientific connotation. The problem of art is the problem of the human faculty through which the artist creates something that did not exist before. The meaning of art is thus directly related to the meaning of man himself and of his activity, so that whether art claims to be pure play, pure beauty or esthetic magic, it can never be any one of these exclusively. The meaning of a work of art does not remain constant, it can change and shift in time, independently of the artist's intention; but art invariably *calls for an explanation of the meaning of man*, it is an appeal to a dimension unknown in nature. The sense of artistic communication is an essential feature of man. If we are to understand the genesis of modern art—more exactly, the intricate complex of artistic problems that have arisen during the last hundred years—we must take into account how man has changed during the period in question. To grasp the anthropological conditions of modern art, which we perceive as changes of culture, we must also understand the related questions of esthetics and of the theory of art, the transformations in art forms and in the social function of art.

I. The Transformation of Culture

It is sometimes thought that the cultural revolution is nothing but a revolution in opinions about art; this is an over simplification. The cultural revolution does include changes in the style and philosophy of art, but it is much more than that, because its social significance extends far beyond mere problems of esthetics, theory of art and philosophy. In dealing with the transformations in the culture of our time, we must remember that the cultural revolution is a general transformation of social consciousness as a whole and of its forms and that it includes at least five basic social processes: (1) the transformation of the content of a given culture, that is, the dialectical process which changes culture in its very essence and reflects the contradictions of the age; (2) the transformation of the structure of social consciousness, especially changes in the particular forms of social consciousness and in the relations between these forms; (3) the transformation of the social characteristics of those who produce culture and of those who consume it, that is, the transformation of the whole cultural aspect of the various social strata and classes; (4) the transformation of the type of man as determined by the combination of all his social relationships, both those which remain stable and those which change, that is, the overall transformation of the historically transient human type; (5) the transformation of the forms of life in society, of modern man's way of life.

In the course of these social transformations of twentieth-century culture, the importance of art has grown to an extraordinary extent. Nevertheless it must be emphasized that art and artists are much more dependent upon these objective social processes, upon the historical transmutation of culture as a whole, than they are ready to admit; this remains true even if sociologism, the school of thought that first pointed it out, is now scoffed at. Artists do not create their work somewhere in the wings while society passes through revolutionary changes, though they may, of course, think they do. They are themselves both the object and the agent of the greatest revolution in world culture that history has ever known.

The objective dependence of art on external social processes must be stressed, not in order to keep art in a state of servility that is jeopardizing both art and poetry, but precisely in order to make artists themselves aware of the nature of the flow of history that sets the limits within which art actually develops, and thus to make it easier for them to assert their inalienable right to their own subjective form of expression, to the act of artistic creation. For the art which refuses to take into account the social process of which it forms a part, and to understand its meaning, is sterile both in its effort to promote the positive elements in our society and in its criticism of the negative features. Then the artist fails not because of the external obstacles that conservatism, tradition and arbitrary power will always put in the way of intellectual creation, but because of his own lack of awareness, his naïveté and his illusions about the function of the intellect in the society of our time; it then serves him right if he is attacked and punished, because stupidity deserves no defense under any circumstances.

This much had to be said, to avoid the impression that we are putting forward romantic ideas about the unbounded freedom of artistic creation, arising from the depths of anonymous history in a self-regulating and subjectively sovereign act of genius. There is no need to return to these theoretical positions, because Marxist sociology provides a much better means than the romantic psychological approach of understanding the meaning and function of art. But these Marxist theoretical positions require that equal weight be given to the fact that art participates in the revolutionary transformation of culture *as art, through art, and in no other way.* Any other approach condemns artistic creation itself to an inner schematism and to a sclerosis of the vital arteries through which artistic thought circulates; nothing more is then expected of this thought than that it produce mere cultural ornaments, varying slightly to fit in with variations in the social setting. Such conceptions of art and its function in the cultural revolution were wrong at the time of the cult of personality and they are just as wrong today, irrespective of any minor modification, or even important change, in the content of the artistic communication. Art is part of the cultural revolution. Therefore it is determined not only from the outside, by the social processes of which we have spoken; since it is itself a form of social consciousness, art, as well as the various art forms and genres, undergoes its own, more or less intrinsically generated transmutations, which are just as unique and without analogy as the social changes in science and technology. In other words, art is not a static and passive object through which social processes act; it goes through its own revolutions and these correspond much more profoundly and significantly to social transformations than they would if art were simply a passive instrument of cultural change. This is the only kind of approach that enables us to understand the series of esthetic revolts and revolutions through which art is passing in this century and which have not yet by any means exhausted their potential, nor even the dynamic growth of their intensity.

Once the specific role of art in the cultural revolution is understood, several important implications for cultural policy follow. It becomes evident that the creative possibilities of art must be broadened, the mechanisms of the bureaucratic management of culture must be clearly rejected and gradually eliminated, and the artist's freedom to create must be respected. For thousands of years this freedom has been and still remains the condition without which artistic creation cannot exist. The economy of a society can be placed under bureaucratic management, provided that the bureaucracy itself is competent, but art, science and philosophy can never be dominated by a bureaucracy, even if the bureaucracy is efficient and educated—which has been known to happen. If this specific character of art is not taken into account, many misunderstandings arise, because the elemental and irresistible process of transformation in art is then seen as deliberate noncompliance with directives, or as an act of political protest, though in actual fact it may be a genuine expression of the very same transformation of culture at which the directives are aiming. It must finally be understood that nonconformity is a constant and essential ingredient of every art, because art is always rejecting the present in favor of the future and always offering man some projection of tomorrow, always giving shape to man's hopes. So the artist is not only a revolutionary in the political sense of the word, he is a symbol of the struggle to give his age a human face, he is man in revolt through his art.

Whether the artist works with lines and colors in painting, with shapes and the articulation of space and matter in sculpture and architecture, with sound in music, with words in literature, with movement in the dance, with gesture and mime in acting or finally with several media at once as in opera or film, *he is always shaping the world according to his imagination, he is creating*. It is not at all clear what the process of artistic creation is, whether the ability to create works of art is inborn or acquired, whether creation proceeds through inspiration or invention, divination or intuition, whether the state in which the artist creates is one of sharpened perception, a clear state of the mind, or, on the contrary, some kind of intoxication, in which the artist infallibly, with the sureness of a sleepwalker, expresses *his own* truth. Artists themselves describe their work in ways which are extremely varied and absolutely contradictory; they suggest that the work passes through the various phases of perceiving reality, grasping the problems, planning, creatively concentrating and actually producing the work. The variety of their opinions need not confuse us if we direct our attention to the essential mark of artistic creation, that is, to the fact, which no artistic or theoretician will ever deny, that the artist does not imitate the world, does not reflect it passively, but forms it and reshapes it, reshapes reality, stylizes it and deforms it. The essential condition of artistic creation is therefore fantasy, fancy or imagination, without which there is no distinct artistic personality. So an artist is not the man who looks like a bohemian, who lives from day to day in a manner which seems abnormal to the philistines and dissatisfies the party representative in his house, but the man who knows how to express his feelings through his art. He must have this ability to a high degree if he is to have any talent, and in an extraordinary degree to be a genius. We cannot tell as yet why one artistic personality is more successful than another, because psychology does not really know what creation is. The man who has imagination and who creates may have any combination of qualities in his character; what is essential is that he have the irresistible urge to create. It is not true that the artist creates primarily for others; he creates because he must, he creates for himself, by virtue of his inalienable human freedom of thought. He may be courageous or cautious, he may break with tradition or hold it sacred, he may be critical or servile, but so long as he is capable of making a world out of nothing through his imagination, the artist, whenever he creates, is a little secular god in the act of genesis. This is where his inalienable human value lies; when he creates, he participates in the shaping of culture, he becomes the actual creator of a private world and a personification of the supreme value of the universe—the uniqueness of man.

If we regard cultural values as a manifestation of the historical process embracing the whole of society, then the course of past and present history immediately raises the questions: What is it that divides one culture from another, why do the schools and styles of art change, what links them together and what distinguishes different cultural periods? There are three main ways of answering, the first stressing the individual act of genius, the second, the dynamics of social relationships, and the third, man's attainment of self-awareness. Modern anthropology conceives these aspects of the historical process as one whole and provides a consistent dialectical interpretation of them. Emphasizing the materialist conception of history, it attributes the decisive role to man's self-awareness wherever changes in the social relations in production and consumption are not in question and where manifestations of spiritual culture, especially art, are to be explained. So the decisive yardstick for the history of art are neither individuals of genius nor revolutions in social relations, but changes in mankind's consciousness of itself, transformations in the way the meaning of human existence is conceived, shifts in self-awareness and self-knowledge—as they are expressed, of course, by personalities of genius in periods of transition. To put it briefly, the various cultures in history differ from one another in the way mankind interprets itself, in the conception of man, in the model against which man measures himself, in the degree to which culture has become man-centered. Similarly, the stages through which man's self-awareness passes differ according to

the specific course of his individual life. What is true ontogeneti-
cally for the process by which the conception of the meaning of
man's life changes in the passage from childhood, through youth
and maturity to old age, in a biologically inevitable and irrever-
sible cycle, is also true phylogenetically for the evolution of culture, for the interpretation of the meaning of man as it is provided by art, philosophy and religion. Here, however, it is not
biological changes that take place but the evolution of mankind,
which is the result of a historical process and of man's realization
of his place in history and in the universe. This is an assumption
that plays a decisive role in any philosophically anthropological
approach to any work of genius, because it enables us to lay bare
the ideas that lie at the very root of the work in question. The
extent to which man knows himself is extraordinarily important
not only for literary analysis but for the process of history itself,
because we have to bear the consequences of what we know
about ourselves, and how. The model of man's knowledge of
himself is not only a model of artistic creation but also to a large
extent a model of human activity.[1]

II. Transformations of the Model of Man

There have so far emerged in the course of history four basic
models of man which can roughly be described as the religious,
the artistic, the philosophical and the scientific models, according
to the method of thinking by which they were created. It is extremely important to keep the distinctions between them in mind,
especially at present when new scientific models of man are being
formed, because no satisfactory result can be reached if we com-
bine methodologies of different kinds, that is, irrational revelation or artistic perception of essences with philosophical speculation and scientific inquiry. But the postulate that the specific

---

[1] The following part mainly reproduces the views of other authors, for the
benefit of the educators to whom this lecture was addressed. It summarizes
the points of view described at length in the *Anthology of Contemporary
Western Philosophy*, Vol. I (1965), Vol. II (1966) and Vol. III (1968).

character of philosophy, science and religion must be recognized has not always been respected in the past. So it has come about that various "methodologies" have given rise to six, rather than four, fundamental historical models, to each of which all the principal forms of thought, the artistic, the religious, the philosophical and the scientific, have contributed in varying degrees, the impact of religion tending to decline as scientific knowledge grows. In view of this interwining of the different forms of thought, our initial classification into four types is too abstract; when we take into account the way in which thinking actually developed, we must distinguish more than four basic models of man, roughly corresponding to the broad periods of European history. They can be classified as follows:

MODELS OF MAN	THE NATURE OF THE CONCEPTION
A. IDEOLOGICAL MODELS OF THE PAST	
THE CONCEPTION OF MAN IN HISTORY	The model of man in the history of culture
MAN AS:	
natural being	The mythical model of man (irrational, primordial)
Homo sapiens	The model of man in antiquity (rational, Greek)
creature of God	The Christian model of man (theological, medieval)
reasoning being	The rational model of man (philosophical, Renaissance and Enlightenment)
animal	The biological model of man (mechanistically scientific, nineteenth century)

B. MODERN PHILOSOPHICAL MODELS

I. CHRISTIAN CONCEPTION OF MAN	Religion as the *definiens* of man

MAN AS:

Homo peccator (immortal soul)	Thomist theology and its conception of man
imago Dei relationship to God	Protestant theology and its conception of man
existence	Dialectical theology and its conception of man
cosmic phenomenon	Teilhard de Chardin's synthesis

II. EXISTENTIAL CONCEPTION OF MAN	Existence as the *definiens* of man

MAN AS:

existence	Existentialism as philosophical anthropology
free being	Early existentialism
responsible being	Existentialism as autonomous morality
rebel and absurd being	Existentialism of the absurd and of revolt
project	"Marxicizing" existentialism

III. MARXIST CONCEPTION OF MAN	Society as the *definiens* of man

MAN AS:

relationship, set of relations	Prelude to Marxist anthropology

practical being	Marx's conception of man
living alienation	Problems of Marx's "Economico-Philosophical Manuscripts"
object of manipulation	Modern Marxism
historical being	Traditional Marxism

C. CONTEMPORARY SCIENTISTIC MODELS

SCIENTIFIC CONCEPTIONS OF MAN	Synthesis of *anthropina* as the *definiens* of man
MAN AS:	
open being	Biological model of man
social being	Sociological model of man
personality	Psychological model of man
cultural being	Anthropological model of man
channel of information	Model of the theory of information
sign-using animal	Semantic model
antientropic factor	Cybernetic model

THE RATIONAL MODEL OF MAN

The rational model of man as a reasoning being has a long history in antiquity, in the Renaissance and in the Age of Enlightenment. But here we are interested especially in the twilight of this conception in the nineteenth century, which was brought about partly by the social changes in European society and partly by the simple question: Does not human reason itself depend on something still more primary? Conceptual thinking, which is part of the process of acquiring knowledge and understanding, is certainly one of the greatest achievements of human reason. It forms concepts, organizes phenomena in series and subsumes reality under them. In this way it enables us to understand causes and general laws. But conceptual thinking grasps only the static structure of phenomena and in fact one of the principal questions of modern science is whether dynamic structures can be mastered through scientific methods based on reason and operating with these concepts, whether it is not rather by perceiving essences directly or acquiring knowledge through some kind of creative hypotheses that we shall understand the world also in its changing, dynamic structures. It seems that beneath the structures of reason there are other, still deeper structures of human mental activity; this has led some scholars to conclude that the most primary human faculty is not reason but imaginative creativity, which is overlaid by the rational crust of human knowledge. Conceptual thinking is the supreme achievement of human reason only because it is a transformation of the primary human faculty of creation. For several centuries, beginning with the Renaissance, the history of philosophy has been struggling through to this modern conclusion, at first trying to reconcile man and nature through the dualism of reason and passion, soul and body, reason and emotion, and the double integration of man in the world of matter and the world of the spirit. But as philosophy developed, it was obliged to see things in a sharper and more balanced focus and to seek a deeper monistic unity. Romanticism was here the turning point. The disparagement of reason and the decline of rationalist attitudes has its source in the romantic conviction that the real depth of the world is revealed not through thought but through feeling, instinct and the more primary layers of the soul. So in romanticism reason becomes man's misfortune and the exaltation of the unconscious is set against the distress brought by reason. True creation is said to arise from unconscious sources and man's inmost being to lie elsewhere than in his reason. In opposition to rational philosophy and nascent science, romanticism exalted other forms of consciousness —religion and art—because it saw in them some kind of emanation of the true essence of man. This was, of course, simply a revival of the religious-anthropological attitude, which again situated the meaning of human existence outside the mere search for knowledge—in life itself, in the emotional sphere. While making irrationalism flourish, romanticism also advanced the great idea that reason depends upon the more primary levels of being.

This dependence of reason can be illustrated by a simple reflection. If reason receives impulses from deeper levels of being, if what determines man is outside man and outside his consciousness, what is it that determines him? This question, which brings to an end the progressive role of the rationalist model of man as adopted by the Renaissance and the Enlightenment, received six basic types of answer in nineteenth-century philosophy. For *mechanical materialism* this deeper, more primary level was matter itself, and insofar as the body was simply a combination of levers governed by the laws of mechanics, the mechanism of the soul was explained by analogy with matter. *Biologism* saw the source of reason in life, reason being an auxiliary organ of life and the spirit being only one form of living matter. *Marxism* sought this level in the social conditioning of consciousness by being, in other words in the sociological relationships connected with the existence of classes. For *Nietzsche's philosophy of life* it was, on the contrary, power and the will to power, will as the dominant feature of man, that relegated reason to an auxiliary role. Finally in *psychoanalysis* sexuality was set up as the *primum movens* of man, and reason (the spirit) was only the sublimation of instincts; the roots of consciousness reached down into the unconscious. The spirit was only a masked libido and our thinking was therefore controlled by unconscious complexes under a surface of rational attitudes and concepts. Freud, of course, remained a rationalist, because he regarded consciousness as higher than the unconscious and tried to gain control over the blind forces of man through the search for self-awareness. This is the principal difference between him and that *pessimist tendency* which in the twentieth century became linked with fascism (W. Klages); this conceived reason as the enemy of life, as an impediment and a parasite, as the germ of decay, which will bring about the death of man unless some regenerative ecstasy succeeds in stopping progress, which is itself regarded as regression.

THE BIOLOGICAL MODEL OF MAN

Man has many specifically human features which distinguish him from animals: he has hands, speech, tools, culture, he knows the good, he laughs, he knows that he will die. Therefore many philosophers long thought that man holds a unique position in the universe, that there is an impassable barrier between man and animals, that man does not belong to the animal kingdom.

The biological, mechanistically materialist model, according to which man appears only as an animal, was first formulated at a time when the rationalist philosophical anthropology had passed its peak. Its illegitimate father was Descartes, who regarded animals as mechanisms; the conception had only to be extended to man for one of the clearest minds of the Enlightenment, La Mettrie, to see man as a machine. La Mettrie did so a hundred years before Darwin, because he could not accept the dualist solution of all rationalist anthropology, according to which man is on the one hand an animal, subject to the limitations of his body, and on the other hand an incorporeal angel, belonging to the world of the spirit. Soon after the physician-philosopher La Mettrie, the botanist Linnaeus took a decisive step when, in 1776, he classified man among the mammals and thus placed him in the animal kingdom. He was to a large extent right, because it is clear even to a layman that living beings cannot be divided in such a way as to put man as a species on one side of the barrier and all the other species on the other; nature does not contrast everything from an amoeba to a chimpanzee with man, but rather the amoeba with the chimpanzee and man together. This tendency to explain the origin of man and then his very existence and his evolution within the framework of the animal kingdom led both to the Darwinian theory of evolution and to its modern modifications, which determine the specific character of the human blueprint through a comparison between animals and man.

Once we base our reflections about man on man's position in the animal kingdom, then the question can be formulated as follows: How do biological species emerge, how are organisms formed? There are only two kinds of possible answer: the creationist and the evolutionist—either they originate in nature, they are given, they are created by God or by nature and they are immutable; or one species arises out of another species, in other words, they emerge through evolution. The second, the evolutionist, answer was already known through the medieval fragments of Anaximander, Empedocles and Democritus, but it was only in modern times, when it was associated with Darwin's name, that it spread with great success throughout the world. But Darwin's main idea was not evolution but rather its explanation, more exactly, the idea of natural selection; this explained the most difficult question, namely, how one species turns into another. According to Darwin, there is in nature a struggle for life, which results in the survival of the fittest. Why do the fittest survive? Because they have slight peculiarities which give them an advantage over the others, so that when the survivors multiply, they introduce slight modifications into the process of evolution. Nature thus mechanically, as if on purpose, selects the more resistant individuals. Darwin extended these ideas to man as well (in *The Descent of Man*, 1871) in order to demonstrate the common origin of men and animals. Like Darwin, other biologists (Huxley, Vogt, Haeckel) were convinced that "anthropology is part of zoology" (Haeckel) or, as the simplified slogans put it, that "man is an animal" or "man is descended from the apes." Darwinism had a popular success and it became a prop of antireligious propaganda, free thought, the socialist currents, and also of Nietzsche's conviction that the line of evolution must be prolonged as far as the superman. Nietzsche claimed that man is not an end in itself but only a stage on the way to the superman, that "man is something to be transcended." The success of Darwinism made evolution the dominant idea of the age.

Darwin conceived the origin of man in an untraditional manner, as the outcome of evolution. His ideas were often taken up in a form which suggested that he saw no difference between man and animals, that he was hostile to culture and reason, that he advocated a return to nature; in short, his teaching appeared as a doctrine releasing man from his responsibilities and classing him in every respect with the apes. That is why this popular version attracted the hostility not only of the churches and conservative circles but also of certain biologists who objected to the subordinate place assigned to man in the universe. They were disturbed by the fact that most biologists saw the spirit as a mere sublimation of matter and man as "an insignificant nucleus of protoplasm in an unstable organic nature" (Haeckel). The effort to restore to man the specific character that distinguishes him from the animals brought about modifications in the theory of evolution; instead of being conceived as the linear rise of one principle, evolution came to be regarded as the multiple growth and ramification of many principles. The most important modification in the way the evolution of species was conceived came with the theory that it is neither an ape nor another man that is the origin of man (Dacqué, Westenhöfer), but man is, so to speak, the origin of the animal kingdom; that is, animals come into being in the course of man's evolution, as a result of the anthropogenetic process. In this way the old antinomy of man's descent and nondescent from animals was overcome; the creative function of evolution is not directed toward any one single goal and earlier stages are not imperfect versions of the present stage. Finally the Dutch anatomist L. Bolk once more modified the theory of evolution when he formulated his retardation hypothesis. He suggested that factors of climate or the failure of endocrine glands in some higher mammals brought about the peculiar condition which keeps man, from the point of view of anatomy and physiology, permanently in the state in which the ape remains only for the duration of its youth. So while the ape goes on developing and reaches a more advanced stage, in man the development is arrested and the structures of youth are preserved. To simplify, adult man retains the structures of the young ape; in other words, man is an immature, "infantile" ape.

Starting from Darwin and his critics, modern biology is again trying to determine more precisely the specifically human features of man as against animals and it is discovering that at least three features distinguish the human blueprint from the animal: man's nonspecialization, the rhythm of his growth and his openness to the world. The animal is strictly specialized, it is tied to a certain environment and conditions of life and its instincts dictate its behavior. Man, on the contrary, is poor in his instincts, his organs are not specialized and they can be used in many ways. To compensate for his weakness in the face of nature, man has his spirit, his ability to provide creative responses to the changing situation; he can adapt to new situations, whereas an animal cannot because of its specialized character. Man also has a specific rhythm of growth, as Portmann's research into his development in the first "extrauterine" year has shown, a specific rate of development in which childhood and a long period of adolescence and youth play a special part. So the biologically specific character of man does not lie in his having a superstructure of spirit above his animal body, because the human body and the human spirit are not two distinct spheres. Man is one and the science of man must also be one, because the old dualist antinomy is not valid. "Es ist der Geist, der sich den Körper baut" [2] (A. Portmann). Finally, the third specific feature of man's biology is that he is open to the world, which implies a particular way of comprehending reality. Animal perception is, so to speak, filtered, so that the animal perceives only what is immediately important for its own life; the animal's activity is controlled by a system of instincts and it knows reality only within these limits, while man is capable of understanding the structure of things independently of their function, objectively. Only in man is there a kind of excess of stimuli *(Reizüberflutung)* which enables him, and also obliges him, to choose among several possible courses of action.

THE SOCIOLOGICAL (CULTURAL) MODEL OF MAN

Besides philosophical rationalism and biological monism, there emerged in the nineteenth century a general sociology, which in Anglo-Saxon countries came to be closely linked with ethno-

[2] "It is the spirit which creates the body." Ed.

graphy and developed especially within the so-called cultural anthropology. From the sociological (cultural) point of view, man is seen primarily as a social (cultural) being, as at once the creator and the creation of culture, and studied in relation to his environment as the whole man. From the standpoint of cultural anthropology, man is conceived as a creative being, capable of determining its own forms of behavior, as a being free to determine itself and to perfect itself. Man is open to the world, unspecialized, only partly determined. Sociologically he is conceived as still more open, as an unfinished task. The two main features that distinguish him are freedom and creativity. Creativity is inherent in the essence of man, in the nature of his being, because man is an unfinished, open process, which forms its own self in a certain way, which has the power to choose. An animal cannot become less than itself, whereas man can either fall beneath his human form or rise above it, precisely because he is in a state of continuous tension, of a permanent rise and fall, because he is constantly extending the whole nature of man, whereas the animal only brings out the potential of his species. That is why man alone has the ability to perfect himself through culture, why only he has culture among his essential distinctive characteristics, why he alone can, through culture, accumulate experience. But once culture has been formed, it has its own autonomous life and man, as *Homo creator*, is at the same time the *creatum* of culture, something formed by it. In human life many things depend on culture rather than on nature; what is regulated by nature in an animal is regulated by culture in man. For example, we have to feed ourselves, but it is up to us to decide how we do so. Thus man is not only a producer, he is also the creator of philosophy, art and science. He is governed partly by culture, partly by his own choice and partly by nature, and so he lives under a kind of condominium of necessity and freedom.

For a long time man was not aware of the fact that it is he who creates culture, and he was even less aware of the converse—that he is created by it. Only quite recently have people realized that they are born into a given culture and into a specific life pattern which their own lives reactualize, that even when they think their lives are completely spontaneous, they in fact grow up in the tradition of preceding generations. People are social, cultural beings; outside society, man may be an animal or a god, but he is not man, because he is himself only when he is among men. So man is at once the most social and the most individual of beings. Man creates cultures of different and constantly changing forms, and his connection with culture, that is, his dependence on culture, is also his connection with history, because insofar as he is a cultural being, he is also a historical being and vice versa. While the bee goes on building the same cell, man advances, his culture changes with time; there are, however, no predetermined norms toward which culture tends, apart from man's own ability to create it. There is no natural culture, natural man, natural law or natural religion, because culture is the free work of man, not of nature. Culture exists in time, it develops; but this does not mean that a plurality of cultures is to be deplored, or that the theory of progress can be used, as in Morgan or Comte, to prove that one stage in the development of culture is necessarily superior to another. The current picture of the world as a continuous dialogue of cultures not only confirms the empirical multiplicity of cultures but also proves that all cultures, and not any one of them which could be considered superior to the others, contribute to the development of culture as a whole. The plurality of cultures must be recognized if cultures are to live together democratically.

Since man is both the creator and the creation of culture, he is also a being with a tradition. People's behavior is not controlled by their instincts, but by the culture they have acquired, because in man the place of biological heredity, so important in animals, is taken over by a cultural tradition, by a certain manner of conserving ideas and experience. Through this tradition we acquire a particular culture, we learn it all, from its simplest manifestations to the most complex. We receive nothing from nature except our biology; for instance, we do not receive speech but only the possibility of speaking. We learn our culture through conscious and unconscious imitation. But, of course, tradition and acquired culture never regulate life in detail, so that man is constantly getting into situations where he has no pattern of behavior to follow. Since no situation is entirely clear-cut, man has to interpret it in his own way and the new interpretation he provides is an expression of himself. Tradition enables man to preserve the values and experience of the past, and so the rigidity of tradition makes itself felt most strongly in those situations where there is no other way of preserving the accumulated knowledge, for instance, in the old societies which had no writing.

Cultural anthropology leads to one very important conclusion: there is no eternal pattern of man, there are as many types of man as there are cultures. But if it is true that we are more profoundly determined by cultural factors than by our inborn faculties, then variability is the law of man and of his culture. As cultural beings, we undergo historical change in our human essence itself, through history we learn about ourselves, we learn what we are. It appears impossible to arrive at a philosophical anthropology whose propositions would be universally valid, precisely because man as a whole is rooted in change, because he is continually obliged to change his face. The only unchanging, constant aspect of man lies in the fact that he is permanently an open question for himself, that the task of molding himself remains his essential distinctive characteristic. Man as an open question lies at the very root of human existence. The way in which the historical conceptions of man have succeeded one another proves that man really is, as Pico della Mirandola said, as changeable as a chameleon or as Proteus, that the essence of man lies in his radical creative freedom, in his potential perfectibility, in his freedom to choose between preexisting possibilities. No cause of human existence is final: only nonexistence is. So long as man lives, he is unfinished, he has an infinity of possibilities and each of these must be destroyed as soon as it is actualized. Man must continually give his life new meaning, "his future is like a spur in his flesh," as one poet put it, he is a living possibility (Jaspers), a

project ("*Entwurf*," Heidegger; "*project*," Sartre), and repose
is his danger. Man is always in a state of being thrown into a
specific historical situation in which he is obliged to choose. Only
if we allow ourselves to become impersonal ("one," German
"*man*") do we deprive ourselves of the possibility to choose, and
thereby, of course, also of the specifically human character of
our personality, which actualizes its own potential and thereby
creates its own reality. Man molds himself, he becomes, he happens, he is thrown into the future, he is sentenced to freedom and
this freedom is his curse, because it is his lot as man. "Man in-
vents man." That is why, in anthropology, dialectics does not
begin at the point where man speaks about changes of model,
but only when the human person conceives of itself as living
change and speaks about that.

All the models of man that we have described emerged in the
nineteenth century; it is these models that explain the conditions
in which modern art originated. The present-day conflict of
philosophical anthropologies, which is being waged, on the one
hand, between Marxism, existentialism and Christianity, and, on
the other hand, between philosophy and science, points to further
development in the art forms of the twentieth century. Modern
art begins with the great revolution in the artistic conceptions of
man that took place in the second half of the nineteenth century;
it expresses this revolution and the new conception of man and of
the meaning of his existence, both of which arose out of the
changing social relations in Europe. The transformation of art
in modern times can be explained only in relation to the transformation of the model of man, which expresses itself through
art. The change in the meaning of artistic creation and the content of the works of art is—among other things—a consequence
of the change in the way the meaning of man is conceived. Theoreticians of art do not need to have it spelled out to them that,
if we try to explain in esthetic, sociological and empirical terms
the genesis of the work of Rimbaud and modern poetry, the
work of Cézanne and the revolution in the plastic arts, the trans-

formation of the theater and music, the dynamism of literary genres, the sources and significance of this genesis, we are always left with philosophical problems which we cannot solve. A new light can be thrown on these problems once we grasp the changes in the conception of man. Anthropological conditions, of course, explain neither the works of art themselves nor the vicissitudes of art genres—or rather they explain them no better than sociology does. The assumptions underlying art are never more than assumptions, however correct and authoritative they may be; whatever the artist creates, his act always remains a sovereign act of creation. In the present extreme situation, when a transformation of art genres often occurs almost simultaneously with a parallel transformation of the social type of man, the truth of this proposition can be seen in the dynamic changes of whole art trends and currents, in the rise or decline of genres, methods and styles, and in the transformations of the forms, functions and meaning of art in the life of modern man.

Conclusion

The modern work of art is a tragic testimony of man's being; it is to various degrees a manifestation of the alienation of man, who must find the key to himself in himself—if he has not lost it. The modern work of art expresses its creator's imagination and stimulates the imagination of the consumer, as can be seen most clearly in the case of an abstract, nonfigurative painting. The work of art is thus the projection of the social consciousness and feeling of its time. But it is not the simple representation of our human condition; it is rather a stimulus to man's insight into himself, it is an incentive to a deeper understanding of man as man. Modern art forms are conceived primarily as a means by which subjectivity, the artists' freedom, expresses itself. This subjectivity as an area of freedom is jealously guarded by artists, who rather infallibly feel that they precisely know that here, in subjectivity, they are defending an essential dimension of man against his enslavement by technologism and scientism, by this modern, universal religion of the intellectuals and masses. Art is becoming more and more subjective and ridding itself of the external ideology and phraseology of humanism. But the process of subjectivization is not harmful, because it is at the same time an appeal to the subjectivity of the consumer, because it stimulates his imaginative creativity and because the idea of art as the objective mirror of external facts is infinitely outdated in an age of mass information media. Only people who assume that the history of art is the alternation of periods of subjectivism and objectivism must see the trend of modern art toward subjectivity as a negative phenomenon; this is contrary to the real sense of historical development, which does not tend to transform people into a mass of little Marxes, but to open for the human personality the door to multifarious forms of existence, which have hitherto been the prerogative of artists and creators. Modern art is a living protest against the world that exalts science and technology, the world in which the whole man is becoming lost and in which history is constantly creating still more menacing situations, as if it meant to demonstrate the truth of the surrealist vision portrayed in the pictures "Hide Yourself, War," or "The Future of Freedom" by Toyen.[3] Naturally, the historical form of this protest changes and the "child of fury and darkness," as one the founders of surrealism, the Communist Louis Aragon, called this movement, must grow to maturity if it is to be up-to-date. But the humanist aim, which the avant-garde set itself when in chance, absurdity, madness, dream, sleep and the poetization of reality, it defended the true, optimistic, unalienated, anti-illusory values of man, endures and remains valid. Man's eternal longing to understand himself, to which modern art holds up a sort of shattered mirror, this age-old longing drives man again and again to art, to philosophy, to religion or simply to thought. In our age, when science and technology are exerting an extreme influence upon our lives, this longing creates, in art, an eternal oasis of the marvelous in mankind. And "the marvelous is the only source of the eternal communion between men" (André Breton).

[3] A Czech surrealist living in Paris. Ed.

Dramatic Models
of Man

[1965]

What a piece of work is man! how noble in reason! how infinite in faculty! in form and moving how express and admirable! in action how like an angel! in apprehension how like a god! the beauty of the world! the paragon of animals! And yet, to me, what is this quintessence of dust?

—SHAKESPEARE, *Hamlet*

"There are more things in heaven and earth than are dreamt of in *our* philosophy," says Hamlet to us philosophers, and that is why we must approach Shakespeare with a vigilant mind, only to discover in the end that he was right. But if we use methods which transcend even Shakespeare himself, the methods of modern scientific anthropology, we can reflect from a new point of view about what is most important in his plays—his model of man. If we want to hit a distant target we need a telescope to bring it closer. But if we want to hit the target in art, we need rather to stand further back, because then we can more clearly discern its outline. History, the awareness of the historical character of man, provides us with this inverted telescope.

The Model of Man in Antiquity

The oldest of all anthropologies is certainly the religious kind, whose model of man is governed by its ideas about supernatural forces and their influence on human life. In the different variants of world religions, in the cultural relics of extinct cultures and in the material relics of still more ancient cultures, evidence has been preserved that the earliest form of man's conception of himself, in prehistoric myth, was determined by at least three decisive factors: a feeling of kinship with animals, enthnocentrism and the idea of dependence on a numinous power. The mythical model of man, which dominates the whole primeval society, forms the deepest layer of every human being since then. The feeling of an instinctive kinship with the animal is only gradually pushed into the background by the great humanist idea that man is something different from an animal, that he has his own place in nature and that this is where his human greatness lies. In his union with nature, in its mystical interpretation, and with the forces that rule it, the gods, man is not a special being, separate and distinct from nature; he exists in a kind of "democracy of all that lives," in the oneness of his human cosmos with the macrocosm of the universe and the microcosm of living nature. Through his union with the tribe, man identifies himself with his group to the point where he acquires an ethnocentric feeling of superiority to every foreigner or "barbarian," and may eventually come to believe that his is a chosen people (Jews, Romans), that his religion is the only redeeming one, and so on. The equality of the nations and then of people is a discovery that came relatively late in man's cultural history. Mythology attained its greatest perfection in Greece and yet it was here that the mythical model of man first collapsed. The rationalist model was created in Greece in opposition to the mythologies. It is distinguished from the preceding stage by several splendid intellectual achievements, the most significant of which is definitely the Logos, reason as the determining feature of the human being. The discovery of this autonomous reason, of the "perceiving mind as the greatest gift of the gods" (Sophocles), for the first time enabled man to understand the world rationally as some kind of order, something articulated, a cosmos as against chaos. It was not only man who had reason; there was also a world reason, which was the hidden structure of the world. Another great idea of ancient Greece was the realization of the stoics that people are equal, that there is such a thing as mankind and that therefore there can be a form of ethics which is universally valid for all men. In other words, man, who has reason, is capable of putting it into practice; he has an autonomous morality, that is, he is a free moral being capable of using his reason to resist passion, to purify himself through passion without succumbing to it. This anthropocentric attitude of Greek culture, expressed in the statement that "man is the measure of all things," that man is his own model, has become the humanist foundation on which the whole of European culture stands. Finally, the third basic pillar of antiquity's conception of man was the conviction that, in spite of this rational structure of the world, there are certain forces which oppose man; they appear as the incomprehensible, blind forces of fate, as the tragedy of death, as chance and the caprice of the gods, as forces against which man's intentions are shattered; they remain incomprehensible to man but nevertheless they are governed by a hidden logic of superhuman dimensions. This model of man's existence as a rational being in control of his passions and yet crushed by the mechanism of fate was most strikingly expressed in Sophocles' *Oedipus Tyrannus*, where the dramatic and tragic character of antiquity's model of man reaches its culminating point.

Oedipus is a drama of human fate; it is a classical tragedy in which man proposes and God disposes, a tragedy of the transformation of human endeavor by a superhuman, transcendent intervention. Oedipus spends his life trying to escape the prophecy which foretold his parricide and incest. Even before his birth Oedipus' parents do all they can to prevent the prophecy from coming true. But the only result is that they all carry out the prophecy of Apollo's oracle; the oracle causes them to create the conditions for the fulfilment not only of these two prophecies but also of a third, which obliges Oedipus to seek Laius' murderer. In the play Oedipus pursues himself and finally identifies himself as the incestuous parricide. It is a painful drama of the road to self-knowledge, the meaning of which lies in this, that Oedipus, the solver of riddles, identifies the man in himself as the unconscious source of evil. The tragedy tells us that in trying to escape from prophecy we fulfill it, so that our fate is inescapable. Man's fate is thus preordained, it can lead from the height of glory into the abyss, we are imprisoned in it for ever. Oedipus does not murmur against fate, but in his extreme despair, when, having blinded himself, he is going into exile, he says: "Whatever you may be, my fate, run on!" The ruler punishes *himself*, he does not turn against the gods; he regards himself as the culprit, he carries out what he threatened to do to the murderer of Laius, whoever he might be. Oedipus pursues truth at the cost of self-destruction, he refuses to stop. The play tells us that people are responsible for the evil that they do and that resistance to prophecy is avenged far more terribly than those who refused to murder the newborn infant imagine. In other words, the gods have their reason, which take precedence over the normal course of events in the world, and people who resist them are guilty. Disaster comes not from the gods but from the people who set themselves up above the gods. Only Jocasta does not believe the prophecies, and this attitude, for which she pays with her life, sets apart from the rest of the play. Her words have a sound which antiquity must have found positively defiant: "What is there to fear when man is after all ruled by chance and you cannot foresee anything with certainty! Live as best you can, whatever the life that chance may bring you—there is nothing else to do." Two thousand years later Hamlet was to take this attitude in his turn and thereby allow chance to play, in a secularized form, the role of the ancient gods.

The meaning of Oedipus is evident: people are the playthings of fate, and if they try to resist it, they engender evil. In this view of the world, therefore, it is people who are the source of evil, not the gods and not chance. The Greek spectator found it obvious—just as the hero did—that he is guilty because he has sinned against the divine norm. But is Oedipus guilty by the standards of the later models of man, too? For the Christian he is innocent, because he does not know what he is doing; from the Renaissance point of view he is the victim of chance; and from the modern point of view he is guilty in that he violates social norms, but that is a cause for revolt against the norms, rather than for self-accusation. When we compare Oedipus with Hamlet, we see that they have one thing in common: they are the playthings of forces which are beyond their control. These are the forces of chance, which are, in one case, presented in mythical garb and, in the other, in the naked form of chance as such. But what absolutely divides the two heroes is their attitude to their dependence on these forces, because Oedipus unreservedly gives himself up to it, whereas for Hamlet it is an absurd, senseless, fortuitous, nonlogical playing with human life, deprived of any metaphysical meaning. The drama of life is, in Macbeth's words, "a tale told by an idiot, full of sound and fury, signifying nothing." Hamlet is a play about absurdity, about man caught in the trap of his own idea, which he created himself; he is therefore more tragic than those who were driven only into the trap of history. Oedipus' actions always have a higher meaning: when he goes to Delphi, when he kills Laius, when he brings the murder to light, when he blinds himself. Hamlet's actions do not have this meaning—and Hamlet knows they do not. Oedipus is caught in the trap of fate and he comes out of it personally ruined and blind, but the timeless norm remains valid. Richard III is caught in the trap of history; he dies and the wheel of history goes on senselessly turning. Hamlet is caught in the trap of himself, in the trap of a life which has lost its value; he represents the total collapse of the human personality, because everything is absurd here: the chance that takes the place of fate, as well as history and man himself, who is pure absurdity. Modern fate is man himself.

Man in History

If we intend to apply these anthropological points of view to the plays of Shakespeare, we must start from the work of Jan Kott, whose brilliant interpretation is so exact that it produces a physical sensation of pleasure in the thinking head. And since I regard his philosophical work with admiration, I hope that a mild Polonization of Czech culture—within the limits of a moderate progress and the law, of course—will make it possible for a tourism of ideas as well as a tourism of people and thus demonstrate the old truth, which was already known to Stephano in *The Tempest*, that "thought is free"; surely in our cultural milieu we can afford to say this, thanks to Shakespeare. Perhaps one day we shall be able to satisfy the physical need for pleasure in thinking from the native sources of our own motherland, though for the time being it does not rejoice in the mild climate of the seacoast that Shakespeare in his farsightedness attributed to it.

Jan Kott has perfectly analyzed the mechanism of history in Shakespeare's historical plays and shown that history is subject to a kind of infernal cycle of alternation of power, where the holders of power change, but the same things in fact go on happening over and over again. Thus history is only the background of history, the unchanging structure of the relationship between man and the world; it is the mechanism of power but it is not the source of anything new. So history is not history; it is the chronicle of events which are written or dramatized against the same intellectual background against which Niccolo Macchiavelli wrote his *History of Florence* or *Reflections on the Decade of Titus Livius*. That is why reason reveals history to man only as a struggle for power, as an absurd slaughterhouse, as a constant tension and struggle, which cannot be judged from an *a priori* moral point of view. Kings are not good or bad, they are not usurpers or philanthropists, they are the performers of pre-ordained roles which derive from their positions, from their *social function*, rather than from any psychological motivation. So history is perceived against the background of a philosophical conception which is equally incompatible with the ideas of Aurelius Augustine, according to whom history is simply the road to salvation, and with those of the medieval chroniclers, for whom history is the *Gesta Dei per Francos, per Germanos*, and so on. History is thereby freed from its theological context, but at the same time it loses its meaning, so that it appears as a mixture of accidents and the activities of separate individuals, as a play of blind forces and as the unchanging structure of the same tune, played over and over again in different keys by succeeding generations. This conception of history is revolutionary from a philosophical point of view, because it represents a new chapter in historiography, leading to the Enlightenment's conception of historical progress and then to Hegel and Marxism. So Shakespeare *a priori* gives up the question of what history means, because the question itself—and so it appears to Macchiavelli, too—is based on a nonempirical, theological approach. For Shakespeare, history is a senseless tangle of human interests (rather like the chaotic dance of atoms which dominated antiquity's conception of the cosmos), because there is no regulating principle which could bring order into it. "History repeats itself mechanically, like an idiot," said a nineteenth-century historian in the spirit of Shakespeare. This conception of history is opposed to the modern one, which regards history as a process, however this process may then be seen. But Shakespeare's intellectual greatness becomes evident as soon as this conception of history is compared with that of antiquity. The drama of antiquity, too, sees history as a mere chaos of events, but at the same time it is also a regulating factor, that which is brought into the cosmos by the Logos, by the order of things, by fate itself, by the caprice of the gods. All the tragedies of antiquity constantly portray the same idea—the subjection of man to a divine order, to fate. This idea is rather alien to Shakespeare, as to Renaissance Europe as a whole, in spite of its great admiration for antiquity, because with the sapping of religious attitudes fate became secularized and turned into mere chaos, where chance and the struggle for power prevail. It is left to modern times to set against Shakespeare the conception of history as a process, as the conscious activity of people.

History in Shakespeare is as cruel as nature, because it is itself regarded as "natural," just as man is. Nature is cruel because it is natural, history is cruel inasmuch as its course is as elemental as that of nature, and man is cruel insofar as he is natural. This is the attitude created by a period of tragic grandeur. The heroes of Shakespeare's historical plays accept this "natural law" just as antiquity accepted fate. Only Hamlet goes beyond these limits, which are the outcome of Shakespeare's conception of history; he refuses to be "naturally cruel" and he mocks himself for it with biting ridicule. His passions are silent because he has subordinated them to his reason, and his reason hesitates because it wants to know the causes and meaning of life (and those it cannot find). Hamlet is an exception in an age which believes that, if a man is natural, he is cruel. *Hamlet does not want to be cruel*; he is more deeply human than the nature that is in him. The historical plays are an exact description of the reality of an inhuman world, or rather the unreality of humanity; they are a testimony about the bankruptcy of morality in politics. They portray the theater of human conflicts, which are insoluble, unmanageable by man himself, that is, unhistorical. Man has become reasonable; he acts, but he is helplessly caught in the blind alley of nature and history. Fate has become secularized but it has not ceased to exist. It has a new character—it is chance.

This tragic image of man's fate, of human existence, is different from antiquity's model of man in that the tragedy of human destiny is conceived in relation to comedy, as a grotesque situation characteristic of man's existence. Antiquity always heightened the tragic character of its heroes, for whom the caprice of the gods set a snare—death or a hostile fate—but man was that heroic agent of his fate, whereas here the catastrophe is caused by a quirk of chance or by man himself. Jan Kott has shown how Coriolanus falls because "he sets up his own absurd system of values against the world"; other figures in history, too, fall for similar reasons, not understanding that they must submit to the great mechanism of history, for the mechanism will not submit to them. Hamlet falls with this difference (so terribly modern) that he upholds against the world his own absurd system of values, the essence of which is that the world has no values. "The most staggering aspect of Shakespeare's tragedies is their suprahistorical character." That is why chance plays with him more and more cruelly; for he opposes nothing to chance, he allows the world to run its course in accordance with Jocasta's advice, and he leaves it to time, "the all-seeing judge," to take vengeance.

Conceptions of Man

But why does history move in a circle and not forward? Another level of Shakespeare's philosophical consciousness provides the answer to this question—his conception of man. For "giants of passion, spirit, character, many-sidedness and knowledge" (Engels) perceive themselves according to the analogical model, which also dominates their vision of history. The essence of man, which is immutable in itself, in contrast to the dynamic surface of phenomena, is not subject to the vicissitudes of history. So that just as Shakespeare reveals to us the conception of history which is linked with the mechanistic-moralist, early scientific approach, so at a still more primary level he reveals the contemporary conception of man as a free being that shapes itself within the limits of its own life. Compared with the theological conceptions—which see man as predestined to salvation or damation, or merely as a miserable, mortal sinner, and closely relate him to supernatural forces and life after death—this conception included that explosive idea which Descartes, Bacon, Bruno, Montaigne and Pico della Mirandola also expressed in different forms. This enormous, progressive, dynamic idea, which marked the beginnings of an understanding of the plasticity of man and his fate, was, however, accompanied by an absolute schematism, which did not admit of a change in man as a species. Man changed only within the limits of his existence as an individual, but his essence itself was considered immutable, like nature, the cosmos, the world. This conception forms the background of all Shakespeare's characters. Man is living reason in the absurdity of history and living change in the mechanism of the cosmos, into which Galileo, Leonardo da Vinci, Bruno and Descartes began to penetrate. Life is no longer a superimposed fate, as in antiquity; even without

gods human existence is fatal. While the basic philosophical outline or schema of the characters remains within the limits of the
mechanistic-materialist conception, Shakespeare was not a materialist philosopher. He was too wise for that. "Shakespeare was not
a popularizer of general philosophy, or if he was, it was only in
the sense that Montaigne was a popularizer of philosophy" (Jan
Kott).

The Renaissance conception of man was shaped in a state of
tension with the previous, Christian, irrationally religious model,
in which the decisive marks of man are his sinfulness, his immortal soul and his faith in God. Man in Christianity is God's
creature, he is an *imago Dei*, he is *Homo peccator*, he is one's
neighbor, he is conceived as the highest stage of being. This return to the mythological base in the conception of man marked
a break with antiquity. Christianity's thousand-year-old sovereign
intellectual rule over Europe, which divides the end of antiquity
from the beginnings of the modern era, the thousand years in
which this religious anthropology held an exclusive position,
greatly influenced the transformations in the conceptions of man
in the Middle Ages themselves; it, also, in fact created the conditions for the Renaissance attitudes. How? We shall leave aside
all the theological aspects against which most philosophers,
writers and religious reformers rebelled. The Christian anthropology had a certain influence on the Renaissance in that it furn-
ished a negative model for the renewal of the attitudes of
antiquity. The rational model of man as conceived by the Renaissance and the Enlightenment, which again regarded man as a
reasonable being, linked up with antiquity and renewed man's
consciousness of his unique value, of the individual as a personality which has no likeness in the cosmos. Man does not derive from God; he has reason, he is capable of learning; and reason
leads man to knowledge and through knowledge to understanding of the world. All these views were known in antiquity, and
there would be no need to single out this Renaissance model as
a special matrix of the way the human race is conceived if it were
not connected with certain ideas which strikingly modify the

legacy of antiquity. First of all man himself creates his own meaning; he is conceived as a free being who is responsible for himself and who molds himself, as is most clearly expressed in Pico della Mirandola's *De dignitate hominis*, where God reveals these words to Adam.

The Renaissance model of man is contained in Shakespeare not as a philosophically worked out system but as an expression of current intellectual trends, as a view of the world in which the dramas take place, as a way of seeing reality. The antinomies of reason and passion, the meaning of human existence and the significance of the human act in history are dominated by this model, and the greater the mastery with which they are expressed, the more they reveal themselves. In the greatest works, especially in *Hamlet*, it is not only the human condition of the giants of the Renaissance, not only the model of man, that finds expression, but also the crucial, absurd limitations of the philosophical conception of life. In antiquity, life brings suffering to man, the gods punish him, their decrees are incomprehensible to him, but the value of life itself is not called in question—not even by the blinded Oedipus! It is only with the Renaissance man, racked by his own indecision whether to act immediately in a state of passion or coolly in accordance with reason—it is only with him that we begin to hear the question "To be or not to be," the question in which the shrewdest analytical, cool and mocking reason comes nearest to a consciousness of death as man's *free opportunity*. Hamlet discovers the absurdity of the world from the same vantage point from which the modern existentialist sees that "l'absurde c'est la raison lucide, qui connaît ses limites." [4] The mechanical conception replaced the magico-naïve view of the world and of man long before this process assumed a theoretical form in the philosophy of the seventeenth century. The mechanical conception of the world represented the secularization of the thinking about world and man. According to Descartes, plants and animals are machines (later La Mettrie sees man, too, in this way), while for man the dualism that divides him into

[4] "Absurdity is clear reason recognizing its limits." Ed.

body and soul remains valid. Cartesianism and empiricism led to the monistic theory of man, which was formulated by the English deists and classically by French writers of the Enlightenment, where man was dominated by passions, the search for happiness, self-love in the spiritual sphere and in which the mechanism of the body was supposed to explain the mechanism of the soul. To work out historical parallels would be boring, but it must be said that Shakespeare operated with this philosophical model of man before its philosophical parallel had been formed and developed.

The most important passages in Hamlet's monologues could be viewed as dramatized versions of Montaigne's immortal pages about death, passion and the meaning of life. Is one to accept one's existence and suffer, or to rebel against the miserable world and perish? The answer would be easy if we did not have a conscience, but that complicates life. Uncertainty about the future constantly obliges us to ask whether existence has any meaning, but provides no answer. Oedipus despaired, Job cursed God, but it is only modern man who asks, "To be, or not to be?" with a cool, factual and terrible analytical detachment, which contrasts so strongly with the same Hamlet's state of mind when he discovers that man is only a slave of passion and a brute. The dialectic of reason and passion, which the Renaissance again revealed in its full antithesis as the basis of existence, should be subordinated to the harmony that man extorts from nature. "For in the very torrent, tempest, and, as I may say, the whirlwind of passion, you must acquire and beget a temperance that may give it smoothness," says Hamlet to the players, advising them to do what he himself does with his own passion. And precisely because he is not a slave of passion, because he dominates it, the conflict can be seen as a struggle inside man, between the different levels of the existence of one single man, not as the conflict of two different passions in a dramatic clash of two people. Logic and feeling contend inside man, and Hamlet's demonic antagonist is not Claudius but Hamlet's idea that he should kill him. "What is a man if his chief good and market of his time be but to sleep

and feed? a beast, no more." What distinguishes man if he is only
food for worms, whether he is beggar or king, and if "we fat all
creatures else to fat us, and we fat ourselves for maggots"? What
else but his comprehension of the meaning of life, that tragic
question which, however, can be answered only by life itself.
Life is a process of decay and maggots are man's destiny. Hamlet's reflections about life, so terrible in their matter-of-fact
truthfulness, reach their culminating point in the graveyard scene,
where they are dramatically multiplied and emphasized by the
fact that the skull Hamlet holds belonged to a man who was once
"a fellow of infinite jest." In the whole of world drama there is
no cry more hopeless and charged with meaning than Hamlet's
"Alas, poor Yorick!" Because there, before his very eyes, in the
skull of the jester he once loved, Hamlet sees the truth of his
views, his own future stares him in the face—and he quite
absurdly speaks to the skull as if it were alive, so that *he himself*
convicts his own conviction of falsehood, or at least of the cruel
dialectic of sense and nonsense. What has been and what is real
in man, what lasts? The process of decay does not destroy man
quite completely, because otherwise he would not be able to feel
emotion at the sight of an earth-filled skull. Shakespeare does not
yet see man integrated in time; he sees only the result of time—
death—and here, too, modern philosophy is beginning to go beyond Shakespeare's vision of man, just as it goes beyond his
conception of history.

The Riddle of Being

Man is—sociologically speaking—a collection of social relationships, and therefore the differences between the types of man
reflect the changes in social relations which are intertwined in
the personality of the individual. But man is at the same time
unalienably an individual, he is a personality which determines
(or rather co-determines) itself, too, and therefore besides the
changes in social relations there is another basic distinguishing

feature in the chronology of human types—man's consciousness of himself, in other words, his solution to the problem of the meaning of life. Philosophically speaking, the decisive measure of the change in the human type is man's answer to the question as to what he himself is, Oedipus' answer to the sphinx's riddle, the answer to the question what meaning life has. The play that provides the most coherent answer is *Hamlet*, because it is the play that most completely and most perfectly portrays the exemplary model of Renaissance existence. Hamlet is Montaigne dramatized, who has been driven out of his castle tower into history and forced to act in spite of his skepticisim. Hamlet is the genius of doubt who meditates upon the value of action and for whom life loses its meaning as he acquires knowledge. It is a play about the uncertainty of life's meaning which, however, is not merely the tragedy of an individual but something much greater, a crisis of values and of the era, the mirror of the Renaissance man in general. Hamlet's secret is the secret of the greatness of man himself, of his tragedy, of his dialogue with his conscience, which speaks only directly to man himself while to others "it will not speak." The problem of the conflicting value of the human act could not have been better placed, philosophically, than by the extreme situation, in which the son avenges his murdered father and where, therefore, he apparently has a perfect right to his act. But direct action—immediate revenge—is constantly checked by the philosophical question of the value of life, which is precisely what makes the spontaneous, apparently "normal" act of revenge by the son for his father's death so questionable. In antiquity man could believe in a preordained destiny, the Christian could, and was supposed to, forgive in the name of the love of his neighbor, but what is the Renaissance man to do, corroded as he is by uncertainty about the meaning of life? Where is he to find the key value when he cannot believe and when the very yardstick against which value could be measured is shrouded in doubt? In a rudimentary form, Hamlet comes up against the enormous philosophical antinomy of the whole bourgeois era, against the whole insoluble parallelism of consciousness and the world, the subject and the object, reflex and act. For unless the human act is organically linked with thought, it is an act of chance—as in Hamlet. Christians did not know this antinomy, because for them thought and act were only aspects of a superior value—the active love of one's neighbor, which was an image of the love of God. Modern philosophy is trying to overcome the same problem by means of the central concept of Marxism—practice, more exactly, practice in human solidarity, humanism. All Hamlet's doubts are tragic precisely because of the isolation of thought from action, because of his intuitive approach to the meaning of life, against which actions appear only as a series of murders, as the alternatives of inhumanity, as the dissemination of death, as pure absurdity. The value of *every* act is questionable once the meaning of life is called in question.

Oedipus doubts only the justice of his own lot. He does not comprehend the incomprehensible, his secret weighs him down, but he does not doubt that his destiny is following some higher, nonhuman plan. In accordance with his tragedy he acts, and he acts royally, because he does not die but turns his action against himself; he blinds himself and sentences himself not to death— which would be an act of mercy—but to life with the knowledge that he is an incestuous parricide. He is tragic thanks to something which is a higher and more sovereign power than a king, he is tragic in the relation of man to the Absolute, whereas Hamlet is tragic in himself, in relation to himself, and to the absurdity of the nonexistence of any Absolute. He is tragic in the crippling of his will to life and to action in general, which really is questionable if there is nothing to measure it against and if it has no higher meaning. The greatest philosophical pessimists of the nineteenth and twentieth century try to solve the same question: If there is no Absolute and if all values are merely subjective, is any value judgment possible? That is why what collapses for them, and for Hamlet, is not only one central value, which could be replaced by another; that is why Hamlet finds not only the moral admissibility of revenge and murder questionable, but the very possibility of making any valid judgment at all. What collapses for him is not his conception of justice or the love of his mother, but his whole self, which could judge, evaluate; it is the complete ruin of the possibility of making any value judgments. Hamlet is ready to bear this collapse of his values because his studies ("words, words, words") have prepared him to understand the worthlessness of his own life, which he does not value; as he says, "Why, what should be the fear? I do not set my life at a pin's fee." And to the world he can say only: "How weary, stale, flat and unprofitable seem to me all the uses of this world; Fie on't! O, fie!" This split between the world and man has long been prepared in Hamlet, by his knowledge, his intellect, his understanding, in other words, by that which prevents him from reacting immediately, which demands proof of the crime. This split is the source of the doubts even in a kind of metaphysical sense; and it is overcome only fictitiously, by chance, by an apparition, by a ghost, so that Hamlet comes to understand that "my fate cries out," and he decides to set right the time, which is "out of joint" and mad. Now he has a new part to play because he has become the agent of morality, of the historical process, he wants to intervene in the course of events, he must avenge his father. But at the same time he cannot give up his stoic-skeptical view of the value of human intervention in history, so that he must act in a kind of double, absurd doubt about the sense of what he is doing. Whenever he is in a position to avenge the fratricide, he fails to act and chooses chance, or rather he does not choose, he flees from choice. *He knows* he should kill, but he does not kill, and yet his whole activity is absolutely logical. So logical that it approaches madness from that side on which madness meets the highest expressions of reason. So he can pretend to be mad and yet remain natural, because the model of his madness appears mad only to those who do not have the key to the deeper level of the meaning of what he is saying. Only Ophelia is nonlogical when she goes mad. So life becomes meaningful for Hamlet only when he is given the task of murdering a murderer; but that is doubly absurd, because it obliges Hamlet to destroy his own philosophy about the uselessness of his own life.

The riddle of Hamlet and the riddle of the Theban sphinx are one and the same, and their solution is man, not only figuratively and abstractly, but also concretely—man as a living existence. This riddle conceals the riddle of all riddles: What am I? Why am I alive?, the riddle which no one outside man will solve for him if he cannot solve it himself. Man is a living riddle, not only to others but also to himself, precisely because he is capable of changing his own meaning. He knows that life has no external meaning apart from life itself. Modern man is a riddle to himself and also the solution to the riddle, as Hamlet is, because he, too, knows that either he creates and guarantees his own meaning or he is absurd. The specific character of the modern conception of man lies in its approach to human life as *practice*, as the subjective activity of the individual intervening in history and in his own life; it is therefore a vision of the world which is not a contemplation of an object but a fully understood human practice, the conscious activity of man. The human life is conceived as the dialectical unity of subject and object, as the unity of man and the world, as a form of existence in which man is always involved in something, in some situation, and not outside it. The subject is perceived in the object, in action. The human being here permanently hovers between objectivization and self-affirmation, between alienation and disalienation, under the pendulum of inexorable time. On the one hand, man is formed by the world; on the other hand, he leaves *his own mark* on the world; he objectivizes himself in work and at the same time has a sphere of reflexive existence. In this sense the work of Brecht provides the modern dramatic model of man, because here we have the most striking example of man as a free, active, practical being and a new model of history as a *controlled* mechanism. Thus modern drama is historically alienated from the chaos of history and the mechanical model of man's existence as a machine driven by his passions, and also from antiquity's view of human history as immutable fate and of man as the slave of the divine purpose. As we emphasize this discontinuity in the models of man and history, however, we cannot fail to proclaim our allegiance to the tradition of humanism, which unites modern people with Shakespeare and with antiquity alike, precisely because it *corrects* Hamlet's famous saying:

> "The time is out of joint, oh cursed spite
> That *everybody's* born to set it right."

Conclusions

In judging the model of man in a dramatic work, modern anthropology starts from an awareness of man's historical character, from an understanding of the changing nature of man's self-comprehension and self-knowledge. The decisive turning points in the history of art are neither individuals of genius nor revolutions in social relationships, but the changes in mankind's consciousness of itself, the transformations in the way the meaning of human existence is conceived. We can see the changes in the conceptions of man if we compare the conceptions of antiquity and of the Renaissance, as they are reflected in Sophocles' Oedipus and Shakespeare's Hamlet.

The model of man's existence as a rational being, dominating his passions and yet crushed by the mechanism of fate, was most strikingly expressed in Sophocles' *Oedipus Tyrannus*. This drama of human destiny is the classical tragedy of man's intentions and the divine purpose, which fulfills itself in spite of man and regardless of him, as inexorable fate. People are here the playthings of the gods, of destiny, and it is they who are the source of evil if they transgress against the divine norm. Hamlet, too, is the victim of chance, but his dependence on the intervention of fate is absurd whereas in Oedipus the tragic life always has a higher meaning. Hamlet further differs from Oedipus in his place in the mechanism of history, in the sort of infernal cycle of alternating powers which is in itself a totally absurd play of blind forces. History for Shakespeare is a meaningless tangle of human interests, it is a chaos of events. It lacks the higher, divine meaning to which, according to antiquity, man must submit. The ancient fate has become the secularized shape of historical chance, while at the same time history remains a simple repetition, a circular motion.

Not only history but man, too, is conceived nonhistorically, because man's essence is static, in contrast with the dynamic surface of phenomena. The idea of the immutable essence of man forms the philosophical background of Shakespeare's characters, who have a timeless validity precisely because they do not portray man in his historical character or in the seccession of generations. Man is conceived as living reason in the absurdity of history and the mechanism of the universe, within the limits of the mechanistic-materialist philosophy of the time. The Renaissance conception of man is at the same time constructed in a state of tension with the preceding Christian, irrational model, because it sees in man a unique, reasonable being who is himself the creator of his own meaning. This pattern of man is contained in Shakespeare as the expression of the intellectual trends of the time, as his way of seeing reality, not as a philosophically thought-out system.

Hamlet is modern in his inquiry into the meaning of human existence, an inquiry pursued in a cool, factual and analytical spirit. The dialectic of reason and passion, the conflicts of human existence, the clash of logic and emotion, the tragedy of death, the absurdity of doubt and action are presented in the play in a manner which makes of Hamlet an exemplary model of Renaissance existence, of the era's conception of man. Hamlet is a play about the uncertain meaning of life, a play about the period's crisis in values, a play about the internal conflict of values inherent in human action, a play about man in a state of collapse and with a crippled will to live, a play about the total bankruptcy of values, about the split between the world of reflection and the world of action, about skepticism regarding the value of human interference in history. Modern man is at once a riddle and an answer to the riddle, like Oedipus or Hamlet, because he, too, knows that either he creates and guarantees his own meaning or he is absurd, because apart from concrete human existence life has no meaning. The specifically modern conception of man, as against Shakespeare's Renaissance and rationalist model, approaches human life as a form of practical activity that modifies history, as a dialectical unity of man and the world, in which not only history but the historical type of man, too, is subject to change.

Man and Poetry

[1963]

Poets create ideas and not realities.—PLATO, *Laws*

Historians of science tell us that in modern science success depends less on achieving greater exactness in the methods of exploring reality than on putting the right questions in the right way. In other words, we have to know what to ask, which question will be productive and how we should ask it. The productivity of the question predetermines the productivity of the result. However complicated the road to knowledge may be, all great scientific discoveries start from extraordinarily simple questions, which may even subsequently appear surprisingly obvious. It is, of course, debatable if the strategy of physical science can properly be applied to the social disciplines, to the science of literature or philosophy, not because we doubt that the scientific strategy is correct, but rather because we doubt that these sciences are really sciences. Leaving aside this pinch of skepticism, let us try to formulate, in a spirit of what might be called a kind of productive naïveté, three simple questions: What is the meaning of poetry? How does the poet see the world? What is a poet?

In dealing with these problems, we can successively uncover several fundamental levels, on each of which we see poetry differently as we look at it from a different angle. Just as a shift in the observer's point of view changes what he is looking at, so poetry reveals itself at different levels when it is examined by a theoretician of literature, a sociologist, a philosopher or an anthropologist. The literary historian sees in poetry the art of the word, beauty and experienced wisdom; the sociologist sees in it evidence about man and about the changes in his sensibility in changing social structures; the philosopher is interested in the cognitive aspect of the poet's vision of reality; and finally, the anthropologist can see in poetry a confirmation of the essential function of man—creation—or even an exemplary type of man's humanity. These approaches to poetry are at the same time approaches to the different levels of the meaning of the work of art. They are classified here according to the general validity of their conclusions, beginning with the most concrete point of view, that of literary history, theory and criticism, going on to the more general sociological definitions, then to the problems of cognition and ending with the deepest level of poetry, at which the poem provides evidence about the existence of man. If we omit the first approach, we shall see that our three questions are put in such a way that each of them calls for a different kind of philosophical interpretation. So we ask the sociologist: What is the social meaning of poetry? We ask the philosopher: What are the cognitive particularities of the poetical vision of the world? And we ask the anthropologist: What is the human meaning of poetry?

The Meaning of Poetry

Not by wisdom do poets write poetry, but by a sort of genius and inspiration; they are like diviners and soothsayers who also say many fine things but do not understand the meaning of them.
—PLATO, *Apology*

The theory of each of the various individual arts usually analyzes a given work of art in a way that corresponds to the conventions and the subject of the branch to which it belongs. This

is the advantage of these theories, including the theory of literature, but it is also their defect, because usually they either fail to
take into account the mode of thinking that another discipline can
offer, or at best they reject it outright. That is why literary historians with positivist leanings find philosophy so provocative—
provided it really is philosophy—because philosophers themselves
detest pretentious nonsense just as much as anyone else. Present-
day philosophical anthropology, which we shall take as our
framework in trying to say something about poetry, has hardly
any interest in analyzing the structure of a poem, in philosophical
minutiae, in essays in literary history and biography, in analytical
dissections of verse and rhythm, or in the morphology of poetics.
It is just as undeniable that these methods are valid in literary
scholarship as that, for the doctor who is performing an autopsy,
it makes no difference whether he is dissecting a genius or an
idiot, because as far as he is concerned, human morphology is the
same in both cases. To discover whether the subject was a genius
or an idiot requires a method which may not be incompatible
with the autopsy but which puts the questions in a different way
from that in which the dissecting knife asks the corpse how it
came to die. What the philosopher explores is the vital issue of
what human meaning the work of art has.

If we ask the authors of the most important poetics of the past,
the Bible, Aristotle, Ronsard, Baudelaire, du Bellay, Vico, Goethe,
Hegel, Hölderlin, Lautréamont, Novalis, Brémond, Shelley, Boi-
leau, Poe, Breton, Rilke, Sartre and many others [1] what meaning
poetry has, we shall find that the answers given by the various
authors, periods and poets are extremely varied. Contrasting
theories of poetry alternate in very much the same way as periods
of creativity and of imitation alternate in culture. Though they
have a certain common denominator, these theories do not permit
us to construct a genetic series in which the understanding of the
meaning of poetry grows steadily deeper, the kind of series which
might be *a priori* sketched out as a development from the per-

---

[1] See especially the useful anthology by Jacques Charpier-Pierre Seghers,
L'art poétique (Paris, 1956).

sonal through the social to a universally human aspect. The conflicts between poetics are usually about the superiority of one poetic element to another, and literary theory merely introduces into the conflict more precise rules and various combinations of classical definitions, instead of subjecting poetry to a new kind of analysis. But philosophical anthropology or, if you like, a more philosophical literary scholarship enables us to deal with poetry as a whole, for it discloses the different stages in the evolution of the types or conceptions of man that underlie the shifts in poetics, while it does not eliminate the conflicts between the various poetics about the superior value of one aspect of poetic creation or another.

We can discover the logic inherent in the development of these poetics; we can, in other words, understand the significance of the changes in opinions about poetry, about its making, its value and its meaning, if we realize not only that the style and structure of literary works, the historical setting and social relationships, have all changed in the course of history, but also that the prime factor, both active and passive, of these changes has been man himself. Behind the transformations of styles and poetics are the changes in the pattern of man. Poetics can remain the same for thousands of years; they endure just as the unchanging formal structure of the works does, and they outlast social formations. The most substantial differences do not lie in poetics or in the formal structure of the works of literature, which has lasted over two thousand years in the form of drama, several hundred years in the form of the novel and which, in the form of lyrical poetry, stretches back into the mists of the past. The essential differences lie in the conceptions of man, more precisely, in the ways he understands and expresses himself. So the variations in the meaning of poetry are closely linked with the transformations of the image and meaning of man in European culture. Ideas about the value of poetry and the meaning of literary creation are therefore exposed to the influence of such factors as philosophy, politics, history and sociology, which formulate the problems of the meaning of poetry from the outside, on the basis of a wider conception of values. The meaning of poetry thus derives from the meaning of man and we cannot say what it is unless we appreciate that the successive changes in European culture also imply a series of successive transformations of the image of man, beginning with the *Homo sapiens* of antiquity, through the Judeo-Christian conception of man as the image of God, to the rationalist version of the various specialized sciences—sociology, psychology, ethnology, biology—and finally to the present-day scientific conception, which has its counterpart in the extremely pessimistic vision of man as an absurd being. The transformation of the meaning of poetry is a corollary of the transformation of the sensibility of man as the creator and the consumer of art.

Before we can apply this principle to the question of the contemporary meaning of poetry, we must bear in mind the specific features of the transformation of man and of the meaning attributed to him. In the past, when changes in poetics occurred, they were usually so slow and so relatively inconspicuous that people could not see that the transformation of poetics meant in fact a transformation of man and of his sensibility. The changes were not a matter of years but of decades, they happened not within one generation but over several, so that the awareness of change dragged lazily through history. What is more, the correspondence between these transformations in the sensibility of the human type, in the historically transient model of man, and the transformations in poetry, was discontinuous, so that the rate at which reality changed, on the one hand, and sensibility, on the other, appeared to be unrelated. As the tempo of history accelerated in modern times, and especially in the twentieth century, it became possible for the first time to understand the structural modifications in the sensibility of modern man and to see them as a simultaneous process of changes in artistic techniques or methods, and in their effect on the consumer of art. In this way it became possible to establish a clear parallel between the dramatically swift transformation in the content and forms of art, on the one hand, and the expansion of science, the identification of social laws and the psychological discovery of consciousness and of the unconscious, on the other.

The meaning of poetry is the cultivation of human sensibility, perceptiveness and understanding of the world. The poem does indeed always mean something in the sense that it has a certain thematic content, it may have an educational value of a political significance, but its social role as art lies neither in its educational nor in its political effect. The social function of poetry lies much deeper, because it does not appeal to any one particular aspect of man, to his reason, his social status or his political views, but it touches the living core of his being at its very roots: it affects and modifies man's very powers of perception, it alters his sensibility. That is why poetry is most radically useful from the social point of view precisely when it is most poetry, and not when it tries to serve society by exploiting its educational or philosophical potential, which is secondary. In all ages, poetry is actively engaged in directly and immediately transforming man's personality, his ability to perceive and understand the uniqueness of the world, and this gives poetry an immeasurably greater humanist value than the possibility that it may occasionally be made to serve some specific practical purpose. And though poetry undoubtedly does have the esthetic function of spreading beauty, it is not confined to this; its greatest significance for man lies in the fact that it is an instrument which "poetizes" life as it awakens in man the capacity to see and feel the immediacy and uniqueness of the beauty of his own real life. The mirror that poetry offers man is the most faithful one, because poetry itself is the mirror of human sensibility, reflecting its own creator, unique, immediately perceiving man. In this sense even the greatest poetry is a marginal note on the process of living, a breakdown of words through which, as through the ruins of an ancient temple, we can see the greatness of life and the greatness of man, the creator. A good poem makes us realize not that we are reading a good poem but that poetry is everywhere man, the immediate, perceptive, free, open being, is; that poetry puts him in immediate contact with life; that it is the democratic, accessible, "public rose" of existence itself. Poetry enables man to understand himself, stimulates his capacity for life and acts as the touchstone of his authenticity; it heightens man's sensitivity to the miracle of the everyday and invites him to become a "fantastic opera" for himself. But if the essence of poetry is life in its immediacy, then poetry resides above all in man's own life process, as an acute awareness of his own being. Without this awareness there can be no poet. It is the most primary level of poetry, which takes on the form of art when it is put into words or expressed in some other way; but in the process of expression it becomes alienated from life itself, because the genuine experience of beauty does not call for words but for stubborn silence. The beauty of nature, of certain critical situations on the frontiers of being itself, the beauty of a bird's flight or of the morning sky—when this beauty is put into words, the text is a reflection of the genuine experience that has been lived through. When all is said and done, from the point of view of artists and philosophers, the exact nature of the experience is unimportant, because its poetic authenticity as a living moment is forever lost, like the time which brought it into being. The poem is a record of the intensity of the human experience. This standpoint, of course, does not exclude the opposite view, that of the readers of poetry, theoreticians of literature and poets, whose greatest vanity it is that they have managed, with their iambic braying, to get into print. It is not the meter but the genuineness of the experience that is the measure of the poem and of the personality of its author, because it is the measure of life and of man's humanity. The poem is monumental evidence about the intensity of being.

Thus, in its apparent lack of function or purpose, poetry is one of the most essential elements in the process of life. Man's practical existence in the world, his contacts with nature and with society are not confined to his productive and political activity. He is in practical contact with himself, too; that is to say, he actively reshapes himself. The transformations of his conceptions of himself are no less important than his productive activities. Or rather, they are much more important, because the meaning of man lies not in his work, nor in his service to society, but in the development of all the facets of his personality; his productive activity in society, though necessary, is obviously secondary to this, since it is a means of achieving the best possible dimension of the human personality and not an end in itself. Poetry stimulates man's contact with his personality, it adds to his most precious consciousness of himself, it makes him aware that he is a unique, ephemeral being, perceiving a unique, ephemeral world, that he is an existence open to the world. And here we reach the end of the meaning of poetry, because we have come to the beginning of the total existence of man, where the poetization of the world is actually only the process which relates unalienated man to the world and where poetry, whether it is written down or not, is an objectivized impression that has been lived through, a pure vision of the mystery of being, a penetration into the essence of things and relationships, into one's own essence and into that of the world. Poetry is the life mysticism of the materialist.

Poetry as a Vision of the World

La poésie est essentiellement philosophique.[2]—BAUDELAIRE

Poetry is not a technique but a gift. Poems constructed according to a system are unsatisfactory, even if they meet the norms that the poet sets himself and carefully keep all the rules *a priori* prescribed by poetics. In a nonscholarly sense we can speak about a poet's technique but, as Byron knew, poetry is afraid of reason. What is essential is not the techniques according to which the verbal material is arranged—although analyses of these techniques are indispensable in the theory of literature—but the poet's vision of the world, which comes first. The optics of poetry, which transfigures the conventional vision of reality, is based on a certain conception of the world, a certain philosophy. That does not mean that the poet poet sees the world through the prism of his philosophy, which happens very rarely, but rather that he sees in the world only what the prism of his per-

[2] "In its nature poetry is philosophic." Ed.

sonality enables him to see. Its distinctive vision of the world, its artistic specificity and its unique authenticity are what makes poetry great. If we leave aside the laws of philosophy, sociology, and psychology, which regulate all thought processes, we see that the poetic reflection of reality has at least three main characteristics which are specific to the poet's vision, to the poetic process by which the poet shapes reality.

First of all, poetry reveals the world through the prism of a child's sensibility. Poetry approaches reality with a kind of naïveté of vision, in which knowledge of the world does not seem to go beyond the concreteness and uniqueness of its surface, the side that is accessible to the senses. This way of looking at things, which is characteristic of the child, is associated with a certain type of human mentality, or rather with that phase of it in which the child has not yet entered the world of abstractions and concepts and in which reality is therefore reduced to its exterior; at the same time, however, this exterior—the sum of sense data about the world—represents for the child an integral, whole, unalienated world. Cognitively speaking, in his reflection of the world the poet deals with reality in a hybrid kind of way, because he uses inadequate means to express the world and his way of seeing is linked with a relatively primitive approach. Insofar as we have in mind the process of thinking (and not its object), the child is a rudimentary poet, just as the poet is a retarded child, which grows older physiologically but whose eyes retain their original vision. The poet sees the world concretely, uniquely, apart from the sphere of abstractions, which do enter his world but leave the integrity of his vision untouched. The poet is a grown-up child.

This metaphorical statement could be substantiated by exact psychological evidence and biological data which show that childhood is a specific (deficient) form of human development, in which thinking is determined in certain particular ways by the biological condition. Childhood is the period of the most dynamic development and change of personality, it is the period of greatest tension, the period when man feels relatively safest in his family relationships, when the nascent personality is highly integrated and when man's openness to the world is at its highest and best. The forms in which the child is capable of thinking and in which it does actually reflect the world are correlated with this biological predetermination. The child's prepubertal development may be further subdivided into several distinct stages according to its age, but so long as the child is unable to enter the world of abstractions, the way in which it reflects the world bears the mark of poetic authenticity, the magic concreteness, the merging of dream and reality, the lack of perspective and the unintentional deformation which delight us in the drawings of children all over the world. Insofar as the poet is a man whose personality develops in an extraordinarily dynamic way, insofar as he remains open to the world, insofar as he lives out his tensions in his relations with people and insofar as he battles for his integrity against the forces of alienation, he reproduces some of the basic features that characterize the mentality of the child and he consciously makes the child's vision of the world his means of expression, or rather the matrix of his perception and interpretation of the reality of adults. But he retains the same poetic authenticity, magic concreteness and intentional deformation which his mature intellect reveals to him in a much richer and more colorful form. Cognitively speaking, the poet is a child who rejects his adulthood.

The poet presents the world with a kind of naïveté, he portrays the world of phenomena while ignoring the underlying facts that he knows, as if he asserted that a stick immersed in water is broken or that the sun revolves around the earth. But from the point of view of poetry, it is an irrefutable truth that the stick in the water is broken and that it is the sun and not the earth which sets. But this naïveté is not for the poet what it is for the child—ignorance of the refraction of light or of the revolutions of the heavenly bodies—it is not naïveté at all, it is simply the immediacy, concreteness and uniqueness of the here and now, of time and space at a given moment. There is a profound difference between the poet and the child in that the child lives in a magic world, thanks to its immaturity, whereas the adult can reach only a fragment of the original magic of this childhood world—and this fragment is poetry. The return to the attitude of childhood is only fictitious, because it is imposible. The child lives in a unique, unalienated, concrete existence, the adult remembers it as the magic of childhood, as a previous phase of his life, knowing that it is a lost phase, past and irrecoverable like time. For man changes in time not only quantitatively, but also in his human quality. The comparison of a poet and a child is simply an analogy, and an imperfect one because they each have a number of features which are not comparable. But it remains probable that, if the modes of thinking of children and poets are ever precisely analyzed—which linguistics should be able to do in the foreseeable future—the *a priori* philosophical conclusions about the immediacy, concreteness and unique individuality of their vision of the world will be confirmed. The poem is a message from the land of childhood, to which man returns through poetry of all kinds. Poetry deprived of its immediacy is deprived of its vital nerve. It may remain a work of literature, but it loses the quality of poetry. At the same time it must be added that more and more antipoetic attitudes are permeating poetry, just as nonpoetical forms are adopting poetry into the range of their means of expression.[3]

The second characteristic of the poet's angle of vision is the specific logic or causality of poetic thinking. At a time when exact science knows and uses the concept of acausality to deal

[3] It is interesting to note that a man's feeling for poetry and its different kinds changes at the different stages of his development; according to the best study of the subject, youth is first attracted by verse narrative (up to twelve years), then by sentimental thematic poetry (up to fifteen years) and finally by the form of speech itself, "the acoustics of the soul" (Novalis), the atmosphere of the poem, the intoxication with emotion. This evolution of the love of poetry from narrative through theme to atmosphere at once expresses and imitates the evolution of man's own emotions. The last stage of interest in poetry ends with the interest as such dying out and being transferred to other objects because the poetic experience is no longer found to be enriching. Yvon Beleval, *La recherche de la poésie* (Paris, 1947), p. 30.

with physical phenomena not amenable to classical determinism, we need not, perhaps, hesitate to say that the poem, too, is not controlled by the kind of thinking that meets the standards of classical logic and causality. From the scientific point of view, the poem is an acausal, alogical verbal structure; the poet does not speak about reality from the point of view of science, but builds a microcosm of his own, he makes something that did not exist before; he is the author of what he has made, he is the private creator of his own world. Logically speaking, the poem is an area of absurdity because here the elementary logical laws of identity, of the excluded third and of proof do not apply. The poet's platform is unproved identity, acausality and internal discord in himself, in his own life process, which he documents in the most authentic way possible, in wild confrontations of words and concepts. These are in themselves nonlogical, because the vehicle of their logic is their author. Aristotle's laws are broken in every verse and in every metaphor. For Aristotle, "whatever is, is"; for the poet, whatever is, is ceasing to be. For Aristotle, "nothing can at once be and not be"; for the poet, simultaneous being and nonbeing is a natural element in the chaos of being. Aristotle determines that "everything must either be or not be," while the poet lives in a state of internal contradiction, as the unexcluded third. In other words, poetry has a different logic, its logic is the elemental dialectics of change, the integral reflection of the world, the antianalytical wholeness of vision and universality of approach which it shares with early Greek philosophy.

From the point of view of exact science, the poem is a worthless thought structure with no logical consistency, a meaningless verbal artifact; but from the point of view of man—a point of view which is richer and more complete than that of science—the poem is full of meaning and deeply relevant. The poem integrates us into the universe, into the absurdity of being, into the chaos of existence, not through the operations of reason and logic, but immediately and directly by evoking the world of values and deeper levels of meaning; the poem returns us to our place among mankind, in an ordered world, in the universe; it gives us back the consciousness of our humanity, which, from the point of view of objective science, is, of course, as useless as what man creates. The social function of poetry is to give man back his humanity.

The logic of poetry ignores the laws of formal logic. Things are and are not at the same time, they interpenetrate, coexist in contradiction, transform themselves in metaphor. So in its logical aspect poetic speech is governed by a conceptual antilogic, by the elemental dialectic of concrete things transposed into an artistic image. The poet knows what he is saying, but he speaks about that which he does not know, that which goes beyond his knowledge; it is in this that lies the human meaning. The poem's communication surpasses logically perfect syllogisms by saying what cannot be put into syllogisms. The poetic vision of the world and of man is based on a syncretism of thought, imagination and fact. That is why in his thinking the poet keeps going round and round his subject, trying to express what is beyond him, in other words, to say what he does not know. The meaning of what he says is always incoherent and ambiguous. But it is this that shows he is human, that provides evidence of the living contradiction inherent in man, for by this means he uncovers various levels of human existence which, like the different levels of feelings, sensations, moods and mysteries, are not accessible to logic. The logic of poetry is the logic of intuition, of insight into the essence of man, it is a proclamation of the oneness of subject and object, of man in the world and of the world in man. The poet's logic must go beyond the logic of fact, because that which is not, which exists only in the sphere of man's longing, thought and hope, is just as necessary to mankind as what exists in the world of fact, if not more so. How can the poet put hope into words except by expressing what does not exist? The object of the hope may not exist in fact, and yet it is, it exists as the future, as a real idea. Factual realism is a stupid doctrine, whereas the insight that embraces both the inner and the outer world and their mutual interaction is a splendid idea, at one with materialist dialectics and with man's being in the world. For it is only in

poetry that people are liberated from their conventional existence, thrown into extreme situations where they must experience
their human uniqueness and importance; only in poetry are they
torn out of the context of abstractions and portrayed in the
actual constellation of the living moment, which is something
no conceptually exact thinking can achieve. This emphasis on the
nonlogical character of the poem is not intended to make more
room than necessary for irrationalism, because poetry is not a
manifesto of man's antirational aspects; on the contrary, it is the
burning bush of truth, it is a geyser of pure reason, which sur-
mounts the limitations of logic. Poetry is thought in flames.

Thirdly, the world of poetry lives in the dimension of the
imagination, which is the most essential sphere of human nature,
the very heart of man. The poet's world is not grasped through
conceptual operations, it rests upon an insight into the given
situation, it is an intuition of the essence of the phenomenon. The
poet sees in images. He perceives the world in the process of
transition. His world is the sphere of dialectics, the sphere in
which one thing turns into another. The imagination does not
eliminate causality, it is by no means the opposite of causality; it
is rather causality conceived unscientifically, subjectively, and
interconnecting the world through links which are based only on
the fortuitous coincidences of living experience, on the acci-
dental interlinking of relationships and on the unique meeting of
things, like the "meeting of the umbrella and the sewing machine
on the operating table." The causality of scientific truth is subordinated to the causality of individual experience; that is, of
course, unscientific, but at the same time it is humanly right and
authentic. Scientific truths did not explain everything, they always explain only something, whereas man explains everything if
he knows that everything always remains unexplained in the
poetic chaos of the world.

Poetry is the process which crystallizes the authentic consciousness of man, it is the act by which feeling passes into awareness.
Poetry is the stage in the process of cognition in which the sense
perception becomes humanized, in which feeling is put into

words and thus given a human character. The sharpness of perception and feeling, however, depends first of all on the uniqueness of the experience; its limits are determined by the experience. If the poet is to preserve the tension which is necessary for poetic exactness—that is, for the irreplaceable uniqueness of the experience—he must resort to the systematic excitation of the sense about which Rimbaud wrote; thus he can attain the state in which it is not he himself who thinks, but someone else—a more authentic man, open to the storm of unique impressions, a "seeing man." Then the words emerge from the depths of the personality and the poem overflows with subjective meaning, it has its own multivalued, polyphonic sense, which transforms the beautiful into the ugly and the ugly into the beautiful. It is of secondary importance whether this state is attained through instant inspiration or through the expansion of inspiration into a more or less permanent state, or whether lyric poetry is created by putting the right words in the right places, with a cold awareness and a suppressed enthusiasm.

Poetry is man's rebellion against literal reality, it is the revolt of his imagination against a given order of facts. That is why conservative people in all ages have rightly considered it as a disruptive force which disturbs the idyllic *status quo*, and an instrument for subverting the established order.

Poetry really does disturb the conventional structure of the world, by the very fact that it introduces into it the human element of the unique, that it is a part of the humanization of the world. The program of poetry is the same in all ages—it is the total liberation of man; whereas the program of conservative antipoetry is always the motherland, the family, property and the altar. Poetry almost always chooses the way that leads to the liberation of man, through the time and space continuum with the fifth dimension of humanity added. Poetry is a game against the rules of the world; it makes its own rules.

So the poet is a man who is constantly in revolt. And he is constantly amazed by the jigsaw puzzle of his impressions, which reflects the joy and torment of existence. His antinomies and paradoxes mirror the naked and pure reality of the world together with mystery, in the mystic union, the *unitas mystica*, of reality and dream. The poem is thus not an ornament of life; it expresses the essence of life and in that way embellishes it. The poet is not an esthete; he is a whole man, he is anyone, he is as essentially simple and complex as any man, he is identical with the anonymous You. The poet proclaims the meaning of life and the meaning of its paradoxes, he creates in the exaltation of his own time, and if he differs markedly in anything, it is only in being more human than anyone else, in being distinguished by his passion, truth and freedom—not just by his poetic technique. His passion makes it impossible for a poet to be a skeptic; he believes in the world and in the value of life, because he knows its miracles. The poet speaks for all men, and only when he speaks for the essential nature of his species does he write well. A good poem is one that had to be written as a human act.

Poetry as Human Act

> La poésie, c'est l'Enthousiasme cristallisé: . . . La poésie est à la fois une science et une passion.[4]   —ALFRED DE VIGNY

People find various values in poetry, depending on what they are looking for—the world of the senses, instinct, thought, faith, feeling mystery, immediacy, wisdom—and it is undeniable that on its empirical surface poetry does provide all these. But they are only the consequences of the poet's personality, which tell us nothing about the actual process of poetic creation, about poetry as a human act. Poetry is anthropologically significant in that it puts us not only theoretically but also practically before the mystery of creation, in that it is itself a manifestation of this mystery and a reflection of man's most mysterious aspects. The poem conceals the mystery of the process by which it came into

[4] "Poetry is crystallized Enthusiasm. . . . Poetry is at once a science and a passion." Ed.

being; or rather, the poem is itself this mystery, in that it conceals within itself an essential side of man. The poem is an experienced contact with mystery. There is no need to mysticize the process of artistic creation, because it is mysterious enough in itself. For the time being we must simply observe that, if we fail to recognize the domain of mystery at least as a sphere of existential experience in works of art, it is not clear how we can effectively neutralize religious attitudes. The sphere of mystery in works of art is the best prophylaxis against the incursions of faith into other forms of social consciousness—morals, politics, philosophy, science.

If we ask specific sciences what artistic creation is, we get answers so poor that they are not really answers at all. The same thing happens if we put the question in a more general form and ask what creation is. It is interesting to see that minds entirely committed to the exactness of science, the historians of science, are on the whole united in their conclusion that the mechanism of scientific discovery, the motivation of creation and the actual process of finding out something new, is mysterious, and that in fact they are capable only of describing the history of these discoveries but not of saying where the discovery originates, what happens in the man who creates, and why he creates. Psychology, biology and sociology simply observe that there are certain correlations between discoveries, on the one hand, and the dynamics of personality, the composition of society and the processes of thought, on the other; but the discovery of the essence of discovery, the discovery of the essence of creation is, so far, reserved for Dürrenmatt's physicist, who proclaims that he is King Solomon. If we go beyond the descriptive sciences and ask philosophical anthropology, we find that the probable explanation joins with empirical evidence to suggest the surprising conclusion that man's most valuable quality is not his analytical reason but his faculty of imagination, because that is at the same time his faculty of creation. Only in the rationalist age of the Enlightenment, which gave it its first impetus to the modern era, did the conviction prevail that reason is the world's last court of appeal.

Romanticism and modern philosophy, on the other hand, raised the question whether reason itself does not depend on some more primary levels of human existence, and it seems that the idea of reason as the sovereign judge of the world and the guide of concrete human life will not stand up to the facts of depth psychology, cybernetics and the sociology of knowledge. But what is more primary than reason? The faculty of creation, fantasy, creative thinking, spontaneous imagination, playfulness. It is this human faculty which is the quintessence of poetic creation and in no manifestation of human thinking do we find imagination displayed in so pure a form as in poetry—if we leave aside pathological cases.

On the other hand, in no instance of intellectual creation does reason fail so surely as in poetry. If we want to catch human fantasy in the act, we shall find the supreme confirmation of man's creative power not in a technological invention nor in a scientific discovery but there, where reason transcends itself, where it goes beyond the frontiers of mere intelligence and where man stands *vis-à-vis* his own creative faculty, before the face of mystery, outside the sphere of mere rational explanations and naked before the silent absurdity of the universe that calls for a human meaning. And that is the specifically human destiny, which is beyond the scope of science but fully within that of poetry as the creation, search for and discovery of the meaning of man.

The poet is not just a man, he is not just an artist of a special type; he also represents the quintessence of the values of human existence, because he includes within himself, in their pure form and raised to a higher power, mathematically speaking, the qualities of the human form—uniqueness, active thought, sensibility, imagination and freedom—which is the essence of all the others. The poet is thus an exemplary model of the human form, because he contains within himself the best possible combination of the essential characteristics of unalienated man. We should not like to paint the present age blacker than it is, but we must recall that the greatest periods of human culture were those which regarded poets as the highest forms of mankind, whether they were prophets, creators of myth or authors of Greek drama. Alienated periods of history, on the other hand, have alternately attributed primacy to the warrior and to the priest, until now our own age appears to have decided in favor of specialized forms of man—either the scientist or the cosmonaut. The twentieth century has chosen not the philosopher and the poet, but the film star, the successful technocrat and the boxer as exemplary models of man. This shift in value toward the alienated types of man is just as inevitable as the future change for the better.

From the anthropological point of view, poetry is threfore an ontologically significant human act; it is the most intimate and the most authentic document of man about himself, it is the most profound evidence about the very essence of man as a species. The poet reflects in himself the essential dimensions of human nature in an indissoluble union. Poetry is one of the forms of man as a creator, who not only regenerates speech in its magic-imaginative function, but who also, with the help of words, constantly re-creates the world according to his own idea and thus proves himself to be not only equal to the gods but also superior to the world of thought. Poetry is the proclamation of human freedom and a means to oppose alienation; it is a confirmation of the basic values of human existence—creativity, freedom, humanity. The true conception of poetry is not that it is a product of the ivory tower, but that, as Lautréamont said, "la poésie doit être faite par tous, non par un"; [5] this does not mean that everyone should be a poet, but that everyone should be a whole man, overcoming the mechanisms of social as well as of his own personal alienation. Poetry is the free act of genuine man.

The poet bears not only the burden of his own humanity but also the burden of his time, its greatness and its baseness, its conflicts and its idylls, its smiles and its tears, its beauty and its squalor. This is what gives the poet's existence its tragic character. Precisely because man is a synthesis of social relationships and the poet is man raised to a higher power, his personality

[5] "Poetry should be made by all, not by one." Ed.

finds itself at the intersection of history and duration, in the contrast of reality and dream, in the confrontation of imagination and truth, in the fire of ideological controversy, in the conflict between the general and the particular, on the borderline between present and future time. This tragedy is a personal one, though it reflects social problems, but it is never exclusively personal, though it may appear to be so even to the poet himself. The sentence which the prince of poets wrote on May 15th, 1871, in the middle of the Paris Commune, "Je suis un autre," not only expressed the young genius' intuition of his personal conflicts; it was the poetic cry of the drama of alienation, which the history of the era of imperialism had just begun to unfold, thus putting into effect the dialectical laws of social change. But the same Rimbaud, who experienced the whole extent of human alienation though he was an exceptionally genuine and homogeneous person (or perhaps for this very reason), the same Rimbaud placed himself at the opposite pole of this great tragedy, both personal and historical, to proclaim another poetic principle of modern society, "Change the world!"—thus coming close to the approach of scientific socialism. The poet is an unalienated man, who bears the alienation of his era inside himself; he is the paradoxical unity of the alienation and the dealienation. The age belongs to him, as he belongs to the age, in a two-sided, eruptive love-hate relationship, the bloody womb of life out of which genuine poetry is born. The poet is a wise man. But if poetry is wisdom, it is, of course, rare and it remains restricted to a small number of people. Since the earliest literary texts, the Egyptian papyri, the Song of Akhnaton and the epic of *Gilgamesh*, poetry has been creating myths, it has been a prephilosophic form of philosophy, the creation of metaphorical parables about the meaning of man. In modern times it has transformed its content and form a good deal, but it cannot surrender its original meaning, which is to make up poetic, graphic parables about man, to create myth. Poetry—and in a wider sense literature and art in general—is taking over various functions which have traditionally been associated with religion. It cannot do otherwise, because no atheism can eliminate from the world the sphere of man's mystery, the fact that man is a problem to himself. Poetry is civilized mythology, it is the "private religion" of man.

Poetry is an image of the meaning of man not only in that the meaning of man is the meaning of poetry, but also in that poetry stands before man and the extent of his mystery with the same wonder with which man stands before himself, with the Socratic awareness that "he does not know what he is, but he knows that he does not know" (Scheler). Poetry reveals to man the secret aspect of human existence itself, and that has been its main function in all the myths of the past. Poetry was the sphere of myth, the domain of mystery, and it does not lose this human actuality because myth does not sound pleasant to rationalist ears. The poet is the creator of modern myths. When he creates, he must be in contact with mystery, because poems composed in the head are bad. Too much reason destroys the mystery of man's being.

Of the poet's words it can be said: "Words from the mouth of a man are as deep water: and the fountain of wisdom as an overflowing stream" (Proverbs XVIII, 4).

Poetic authenticity is also rooted in its means of artistic expression—in language. Unlike the artists working with other media, with tone or gesture, the poet has the command of his medium by the very fact that he is a human being. Poetry is the most natural of the arts, the best stylized and the most genuine form of expression, appealing to man's inborn knowledge of the world and of himself through the means which are the most widespread and universal—words. And just as speech is undoubtedly one of the features that make the human species human and represents the summit of intellectual development, so the summit of speech is not logic but poetry. Lyrical poetry is the maximum concentration of man's humanity.

Poetry is the expression of human values in their crystalline purity, it is the most important stamp of humanity (anthropinon), it is the supreme creation of man's faculties, it is the most valuable product of the process of humanization. The poem is the expression of unalienated, whole, genuine, creative, free man. What our time needs then, filled as it is with alienation, mutilation of personality, depersonalization, misrepresentation and restraints is more poetry.

Theories of
Alienation

[1965]

The resistance must of course be adapted to the structure of
the totalitarian system, otherwise it would be naïve. Manly honor
before the thrones of kings is quixotic when what a man is up
against is not the thrones of kings but totalitarian apparatuses.
Resistance must nest in the dead corners [*in den toten Winkeln*]
of the system . . . where the system shows cracks and fissures,
and try to broaden them by subversive methods. Here the sus-
picion that even insignificant signs of resistance may reflect a
very radical intention is objectively justified. Every skepticism,
however slight, really means total opposition, even the slightest
damage is total sabotage. [Hans Freyer]

Classification of Theories

1. The philosophical term for modern human evil is "alienation."
Hackneyed and fasionable, ideological and speculative though it
may be, this term designates what is in fact the specific problem
of man in our century. Alienation is connected with a certain
conception of man and its origin can therefore be explained only
in the context of a certain anthropology. The theory of alienation is based on a certain theory of man; therefore the interpretations of the origin of alienation and of the way to overcome it
depend upon the theory of man from which they start.

2. Theories of alienation can be classified *according to the
methods* (and the theories of man) on which they are based or

according to their fundamental approach to the nature of alienation. According to the methodologies (and the anthropological
starting points related to them) we can distinguish four basic
types of theory: *(a) the theological type*, the methodology of
which presupposes transcendence; it is divided into several
schools of varying sizes according to the religion or faith that
determines the conception of man (Tillich, Barth, Brunner,
Buber, the Zen masters); *(b) the philosophical type*, the methodology of which consists in rationalist speculation, and which
may also postulate transcendence provided it does not interfere
with the rational process; this type is again divided into a series
of schools, the most significant of which are existentialism, Marxism and positivism; *(c) the scientific type*, which is empirical in
its methodology and does not presuppose transcendence; it is
divided into four principal branches according to the scientific
discipline from which it draws its empirical data: sociology, psychology and social psychology, biology, anthropology and cultural anthropology; *(d) the artistic representation* of man's alienation, which is not based on any theory and therefore, strictly
speaking, does not enter into this classification, but which nevertheless plays an important part in the work of Joyce, Céline,
Kafka, Proust, modern poetry, etc.

3. Most theories of alienation, and even attempts to reproduce
the views of earlier thinkers, ignore the qualitative differences
between the methodologies that are organically bound up with
the theories. The various *types* of theory of alienation cannot be
compared with each other because they operate with different
a priori assumptions and methodologies. The truth of the theological type cannot be compared with the truth of the philosophical
type, just as the faith of the mystic cannot be compared with
rational proofs of the existence of God, though in both cases the
authors may have had the same end in view. To mix different
methodologies together is against the rules of thought. The
philosophy that criticizes theological assumptions about man and
his alienation is just as invalid as the theology that criticizes the
speculative and rationally deduced conclusions of philosophy.

Once *a priori* truth or salvation is attributed to one methodology, any dialogue becomes impossible, because it essentially turns on both sides into a confused proclamation of faith—in reason, in God, in humanism or in the apparatus.

4. Only empirical science provides an objective basis for discussion, but this should not be dragged into ideological disputes, because there it would cease to be science. The scientific, empirical, view simply notes that there are three ideological (non-scientific) types of theory of man and of alienation, and the question of their veracity and especially of their redeeming power simply does not arise. Even this approach has its negative aspects, because it subjects man and his alienation to an analytical scrutiny that breaks up the whole and destroys it. Science always tends to isolate the sociological, psychological, biological or other aspects and to take the partial picture of alienation or of man for the whole. But this obstacle can be overcome when the development of the theory of man and his alienation reaches the stage of synthesis, while ideology in all its variants, whether Christian, Zen Buddhist, materialist, idealist, authentically artistic or symbolist, creates obstacles that are insurmountable.

5. Within each type there are many variations, which derive their names from individual existentialists, Marxists, Freudians, neo-Freudians, social psychologists.

6. If we apply a different criterion to the theories of alienation and classify them *according to the results of the analysis* rather than according to methodology, we find that (1) alienation is seen as *the eternal lot of man*, in other words, as a kind of philosophical *anthropinon* or distinctive feature of man, so that the question of overcoming it has no meaning; man is alienated from God, from the Absolute or from society by the very fact that he is man; this view predominates in the religious attitude, where alienation is linked with original sin; (2) alienation is further seen as *a historical category* of the civilized life of man and its transformations are determined by the given period, culture and socio-economic conditions; history is then the history of human alienation; this view is most perfectly developed by Marx, who links

the overcoming of alienation with the disappearance of the civilization of societies based on class distinctions; (3) alienation can finally be seen as *the specific expression of twentieth-century man*, in other words, as a new historical phenomenon, related especially to the development of science and technology with its social repercussions, to the revolution in warfare and to the possibility of man's annihilation.

7. Next, we can classify theories of alienation according to their view of *what man is alienated from*, that is, whether the decisive "evil," sin, danger or error is taken to lie in the abyss between *(a) man and God, (b) man and society*, or *(c) man and his own personality*. If we simplify these three principal divisions we can roughly say that (a) in the theological view, the predominant methodological assumption is transcendence, alienation is the eternal lot of man, arising from original sin, and man is alienated from God; *(b)* in the philosophical view, the predominant conception of man is rationalistic, alienation is historically determined, and it can be overcome through the discovery of a harmonious relation between man (as individual) and society; *(c)* in the scientific view, man is conceived empirically, as the bearer of a series of different roles, alienation is seen as the result of technological development and the solution is held to lie in science.

8. The theory of alienation as modern evil therefore depends upon one's final approach to the question of human values, upon an idea of the aim that man pursues in life, in other words, upon one's idea of human happiness. There are no ideologies that *desire* evil and unhappiness, they all want the good and happiness, but they find them in different forms of existence. Some ideologies see happiness in the welfare of a race, nation, or class, that is, of a group to which the individual is to subordinate himself, others in the happiness of the individual seen as salvation, as the development of the personality, as material well-being or as pleasure. The very variety of these conceptions creates the possibility of conflict, because each ideological party tends to consider the happiness of the other parties as evil and as a threat to

its own happiness. The second sphere of conflict arises from the problem of achieving the final end of man, that is, from the question of which means are to be used. Wars between Christian states were just as much a matter of course as are the probable conflicts between states with a Marxist orientation.

9. Finally, even if there is agreement about means, conflicts arise in the practical pursuit of the ends, in action, in human behavior. So ideologies differ substantially one from the other in their conception of man and his happiness, in their methods of manipulating people and in their actual practice. From the non-ideological, scientific point of view, the only relevant issue is whether an ideology is tolerant and seeks only to persuade others, or whether it is willing to go to war in order to make the "unhappy" part of humanity happy according to one of the possible conceptions of happiness. Scientifically speaking, the basic human needs are known and their satisfaction does not create any theoretical problems; once they have been satisfied, our views about happiness are, after all, irrelevant. Man needs to survive, to be integrated in some group and to find security in some stable order. If we were satisfied with this view—it is factually justified and correct—we should have to feel sure that civilization will bring a further growth of knowledge and produce changes in the structure of society and in political relationships, that science itself will transform society. "Scientists of the world must unite" (Einstein).

10. The scientific view is unfortunately too naïvely optimistic because its conception of history as the mere growth of human knowledge is *one-sided*. The development of civilization is influenced by other factors and indeed the decisive factor of modern history is not so much science as technology. The élite of world science frequently proclaim that the chief enemies of knowledge—intolerance, resignation and fear—must be fought, and they are, of course, right. But at the same time almost all scientists of the positivist, scientistic, antiphilosophical school forget to add that these traditional approaches to the enemies of science are an anachronism if they are isolated from the social

context. The traditional ways are not viable, we need new solutions based on an understanding of the realities of the world of today. These solutions may, but need not, be in agreement with tradition (the old Judeo-Christian or the new Marxist tradition), they may, but need not, be based on nontraditional attitudes with open horizons and solutions, they may be ideological or non-ideological. What is decisive from the scientific point of view is whether they help to produce rationally justifiable principles of coexistence, whether they do, or are likely to, lead to war and whether the methods they propose to follow tend rather to satisfy than to frustrate the basic needs of man. *This can be determined with absolute objectivity*, whereas every ideology, on the contrary, tries with all its power to destroy the possibility of an objective comparison.

11. It is impossible to share the scientific enthusiasm for pure science without reservations. Science is the only way we have of learning about the crises of our country; ideologies have been discredited even among the masses for which they were constructed, and religion may offer us personal salvation but it will not deliver us from the problems in which the world is trapped. Problems of knowledge are only one aspect of the difficult situation that must be solved. The fact that a certain group of people recognizes the principles of rational knowledge, peaceful coexistence and nonviolence does not necessarily mean that these principles will be put into effect. The problems of our time will not be solved through the practical application of science, as scientists generally believe, nor through the simple growth of man's technical know-how in the conquest of nature. Scientists are terribly mistaken when they identify the interests of science with the interests of man and when they assume that people will act rationally, in a way which can be proved objectively to be reasonable. On the contrary, it is becoming more and more obvious that the growth of science and the application of science in society depend on certain social changes and processes, in other words, on politics.

12. Einstein once wrote that the discovery of nuclear fission

is not necessarily any more dangerous than the discovery of matches. This was his way of expressing the common myth that technology is neutral in itself and that it depends only on society whether it will use technology for the good of mankind or to harm it. This is again logically correct, but it fails to take into account the fact that technology is part of the life environment of modern man, that it is a force which determines modern society in certain ways which transforms technology into a new quality. The atom bomb, brainwashing, birth-control pills and satellites are neutral only on the plane of pure thought, but not as social facts. Technology may ally itself not with science but rather with myth, with imperialist ideology or with religion, especially in countries where it has only been imported and where science itself has no independent intellectual tradition.

13. Scientism is not enough, and the ideologies that form politics are fakes. We must think scientifically, that is, internationally, without illusions and truthfully about the situations in which we find ourselves, and if we do not want to neutralize the possibility of action, we must accept the fact that masses of people are dominated by ideology. It seems unrealistic to me to fight one ideology by another, whether it is revisionism or Christianity. Let us therefore understand what is happening in the world and let us act in the way that furthers the basic, objectively verifiable values and interests. Let us do so regardless of ideologies, that is, regardless of whether we find ourselves in agreement or in conflict with them. Let us think internationally, let us approach the big problems with the necessary degree of objectivity and let us rely on the hope that modern technology, which has unintentionally created a common fate for all mankind, will help to bring about certain rational solutions, not only in industry but also in human relations.

The Sources of Alienation

14. Finally, we can classify theories of alienation *according to their starting point*, that is, according to the reason they give for

the impoverishment of the human personalities and their alienation from society. But what we see as the source of alienation
again depends on how we regard the nature of alienation and of
man, so it is only to be expected that the conception that sees
man primarily as a producer relates his alienation to his work
activity or to technology, those which see man as a social being
seek the source of his alienation in the political regime and the
social structure, the psychologically oriented conceptions of man
find the source in individual or social psychology and finally the
transcendentally oriented conceptions see it in man's loss of God
or in original sin.

15. This classification of the theories of alienation produces
the following overall picture:

The source of alienation is

(a) *the essence of man,* the human condition, and alienation is a
natural state;

(b) *individual psychology,* human consciousness, and alienation
is a certain mental state of psychological or moral failure, it
is the alienation of man from himself;

(c) *the loss of God,* an insufficient "linking back" (*re-ligio*) of
man to the universe, and alienation is then the socially psychological state of whole social groups, that can be overcome again by the spread of religion, philosophy, the arts,
that is, by a change in social awareness;

(d) *technology,* especially military technology, the fact that
people are losing control of machines; alienation is the state
in which people are dominated by technology and threatened by nuclear disaster;

(e) *the political regimes of totalitarian states,* which reproduce
the state of unfreedom on a mass scale, and alienation is then
the restriction of basic human civil rights;

(f) *the social structures of industrial societies,* which create a
conflict between society and the community; the alienation
of man is due to the fact that is only a part of the system's
mechanisms;

(g) *the fetishism of commodity production,* that is, the social structure of class society, which creates the alienation of the production process and then of the other aspects of human existence.

16. Marx's is still the most far-reaching and profound of the theories of the alienated society, because it integrates the various individual aspects of alienation in one coherent intellectual construction. For Marx, as for Hegel, history is the development of different forms of alienation; he evolves a philosophy of history in which history is conceived as the secular movement of productive forces and production relations. This aspect of Marxism, the dialectics of human alienation, has attracted great interest in recent years, but only because Marx has been misunderstood and misrepresented as a mere theoretician of alienation, which he never was. His emphasis on the practical way out of alienation, through social activity, through personal practice, through man's participation in history, through his sharing in the revolutionary process that transforms social relations, of course remains unnoticed, so that the meaning of Marx's effort to change the world is substantially distorted. Marx thus reduced and tamed can be discussed anywhere, at any time, and nobody will be offended. Yet it was the fear of this Marx that led the dogmatic school to maintain, even quite recently, that there is no alienation in socialist society and that it is a pseudo-problem of the West.

17. With whatever degree of objectivity and according to whatever theory it is analyzed, alienation is the most urgent problem facing the industrial societies of West and East alike. The term itself so discredited by journalism, may be abandoned, but the human problems that make up the phenomenon it designates will remain. The important thing, therefore, is not the term "alienation" but the human reality to which it refers, man's situation in modern industrial society with its continual process of change, both in the West and in the East. The forces of alienation have existed at all times, under all social systems, in every period of history, and the development of civilization is the apparently constant growth of the alienation. But the decisive fact is that the "forces of alienation," which have always existed, to-

day predominate, that they determine the temper of the times, actually threaten the existence of man as a species and jeopardize the freedom of entire societies. Man is the prisoner of the apparatuses of civilization and in his imprisonment he changes the basic conditions of his existence themselves. Though man's fear of this transformation, which must necessarily have a social character, may be associated with his relative prosperity, that does not change the substance of the matter. The extent to which the very foundations of human existence are changing is comparable in its significance only to the transition from the roving life of the hunters to that of the settlers, in other words, with a fundamental transformation of culture and civilization, not with a mere change of social order or political system.

18. Alienation is in fact the name given to various totally distinct aspects of the global process of transformation through which mankind is going in the present age, seen from a purely negative point of view, as the loss of certain features that earlier man possessed. In reality the process of transformation is ambivalent, destroying one set of values and creating another, it modifies our scale of values and changes the manner of our existence. So it is *a priori* wrong to see alienation as an isolated process, as some kind of fall of man; that is only a conceptual, metaphysical construction, with a hidden ideological content. It would lead us to see in the rise of the urban civilizations of the ancient East a process of alienation and a falling away from the values and styles of life of the settled shepherds, which was more "natural" and closer to nature, but which in its turn would represent a decline from the state in which we sat in our caves gnawing bones, not yet alienated from nature's embrace, though even this would be a decline from the time when we went about on all fours. Such a view of the course of alienation is in reality a secularized version of the doctrine of original sin, it is the theory of evolution in reverse. Of course, it is not usually put forward in the extreme form, but it can be seen to underlie the condemnations of modern societies and in the simplified, incomplete theories of alienation. The romantic illusion of the "natural" man,

good by nature and spoiled by civilization, Rosseau's anticultural and questionable myth, has thus found its expression. Perhaps it may now also find its own encyclopedists who will not only express their revulsion against the negative aspects of man's transformation in emotional terms, but who will also grasp it rationally and practically.

19. The protest against alienation and the pseudo-criticism of industrial society—so common, so fashionable and so eagerly accepted today—only create confusion so long as they confine themselves to the area already accepted by ideology. The criticism that only skims the surface of political life or of the social structure is much worse than the informed conformism that understands the processes of transformation. The critic who criticizes only what may be criticized is not criticizing at all. Critical nonconformism has an intrinsic value, but its real worth depends on the extent to which it has understood what it is criticizing. It is very important to discriminate between the various kinds of criticism at a time when even government dailies are being critical in their way. The changes in socialist society are giving rise to a series of critical illusions, the most important of which is, that the illusion of tolerated criticism is not an illusion. If we look back, we see that criticism progressively came to be tolerated so long as it was applied to capitalist society, then to representatives of capitalism, then, in the transitional period, to representatives of socialism who were held to be traitors, then to representatives of the cult of personality provided they were sufficiently low-placed, then, sometimes, exceptionally, to district secretaries and, of course, unofficial criticism dares to go even higher. Criticism meant criticism of personalities, not an analysis of the issues. It never went so far as raising the one substantive issue—the organizational defects of the social structure—which Togliatti raised in the summer of 1956 as the problem of the source of the cult of personality and which Czech philosophers, too, were asking themselves at the time—and not with impunity.

20. The criticism of alienation is useful even if it deals only

with partial aspects, provided it is based on the understanding that the process of transformation changes whole political, productive, social, psychological and personal structures so that a given process which appears to be negative need not in fact be so at all, because it may simply be the dying off of barren branches to which we wrongly attribute certain values. The criticism of responsible personalities must not blind us to the much more essential kind of criticism—that of the politicoeconomic structures. It does not matter, after all, *who* it is who governs, or rather what personalities perform the governing function; what is important is *how* he governs, that is, within what limits he can govern and *if* anybody actually does govern. The criticism of the human problems of socialist society has now begun to go deeper, in the sense that it is taking into account not only the political configurations of governing personalities, but also the structure of this society, so far as its economic side, at least. But the only true criticism is that which transcends mere theory, which sees the dialectic of modern history as the process in which society and man are transformed, and which calls man to take practical action and to overcome his alienation. Thus we come to the problem of the new humanism.

The Dialectical Conception

21. All theories of alienation (except the ontological) start from the premise that such a thing as alienation exists and therefore can be changed, and that external forces—whether it be technology, God or the regime—are depriving man of the opportunity to develop fully. Alienation always means the impoverishment of man's humanity; it is secondary whether man is seen as a being fragmentary in itself or split by external forces, subject to self-alienation or deformed by the process of production, by lack of faith in God or by the nuclear threat. Alienation therefore designates a certain lack of humanity while it presupposes a norm of humanity, that is, a certain model in relation to which

a given man, group of men or society is alienated. Alienation presupposes an *a priori* knowledge of the norm from which man is alienated, that is, of the human model compared with which every alienation represents a defective image of man. But does such a norm actually exist? Is there such a thing as an authoritative standard of man?

22. There is such a norm, but only in ideology. All theories of alienation have a hidden ideological character, because they argue in favor of their conception of man, which claims to overcome alienation, and they do so rather effectively, because man feels the inadequacies of his own personality, of his social group or of his social relations and he is looking for a solution. He meets ideologies which claim that they have the cure for his aliena- tion—in faith in God, in enrollment in a political party or in psychotherapy. They do not help to convince him that he is a free person, capable of solving his own human problems, but persuade him that he is an unfree being requiring ideological sup- port. Ideologies pretend that they know man's mission on earth, so that alliance with them removes man's uncertainty about the meaning of his own life. Thus all ideologies postulate a certain standard of human experience and then judge man according to how well he measures up to it. So man suffers from alienation be- cause he does not believe in God or because he is frustrated, and he does not suffer from it if, for instance, he attends meetings or supports the pacifist stand on war.

23. Man can be alienated from his human essence only if he has one to begin with. But whether man has an essence, a sub- stance that is unchanging and objectively knowable, is highly controversial even for the ideologies and philosophical systems themselves. Man can be alienated only if this "essence of man" exists, because, if it does not, the very concept of alienation is irrelevant and no more than a secular myth about Adam's exile from paradise, in other words, a speculation in mundane terms about the sinful separation of man from God, nature or society; at the same time the authors of these speculations are themselves unaware of their mythical character. But as soon as we come up

against the question of human essence, we immediately meet three substantive objections, which strike at the very roots of the concept of alienation and which oblige us to give up the term itself entirely, though not to give up the real problems that it conceals.

24. The first objection is formulated by existentialism, which assumes that man is a changing being, that he has no fixed essence, that he is free to form himself and that he cannot therefore shift the responsibility for his alienation anywhere outside himself. Man has no essence precisely because his essence is freedom. This view also corresponds to the newer conceptions of the relations between essences and phenomena. According to these, it is no longer possible to assume that there exists a norm of the true essence of man, in relation to which actual people are only phenomena of alienation. Man's tragic destiny is his own doing, it is the result of his own decisions and not of his wandering in some heteronomous morality in which he is an alienated being seeking salvation. The second main objection arises from the standpoint of contemporary science, which sees man as an open being, as an open structure of human experience, as a series of changing forms of existence, and the question of man's essence does not arise and has no meaning, because science deals only with the world of fact, not with a dual world of essences and appearances. Man is an open being with certain specific features; whether these findings concern appearances or essences is left to ideologies, religions and people's own estimation to determine. The third objection comes from the sphere of Marxism, which does presuppose an "essence of man," but conceives it as a process of change, as a dialectic of existence. Man's factual freedom of action, his practice, therefore neutralizes alienation, just as the sequence of the phenomenal (historical) images of man and his phases neutralizes the traditional view of essence. "The essence of man is man himself" (Marx).

25. These philosophical objections to the idea of an unchanging essence of man are not only intellectually consistent; they find a still stronger support in the objective social processes of the twentieth century, namely, (1) the transformation of human

reality (the world); (2) the transformation of the social situation, the *state* (the relationship between the individual and society); and (3) the transformation of the human type (the anthropological transformation). These fundamental arguments of history itself must be examined more closely, also because they are usually almost ignored in reflections about man, though it is precisely these essential changes in human existence that give rise to the theoretical explanations of alienation. The objective social movement of history is the basis of man's awareness of the world and of the transformation of the world.

26. By the changing nature of human reality we mean the radical transformation of man and society, the permanent revolution caused and renewed by the enormous expansion of mankind's productive forces and made possible by the exploitation of science and technology in the process of production. This universal social transmutation produces entirely new conditions in the human scene. It creates new centers of civilization outside Europe and leads to the widespread urbanization of the population and the expansion of big cities, the industralization of hitherto preindustrial societies and the rise of international conflicts leading to the permanent threat that mankind will be annihilated in a nuclear holocaust. These objective historical processes are now being accelerated by the population explosion with its threat of starvation and by the acquisition of nuclear weapons by other great powers, so that all over the world they are bringing about profound structural changes. On the one hand, there is the rise of élites composed of the representatives of political bureaucracy, military machinery and economic capital; on the other hand, masses of people are being turned into manipulated objects. They must, of course, be given a mass culture of housing, television sets and cars, so that smiling robots may easily be dominated by mass entertainment media and may thus willingly accept the fetishes of the élite and its factual power.

27. A hundred years ago Karl Marx brilliantly foresaw the revolutionary transformation of social relations and the role to be played in it by the masses of the industrial societies. The sub-

stance of his conception of society, history and man is the most profound philosophical basis for an anlysis of present-day society and it is now universally recognized as such, even among his most fervent opponents. But Marx was mistaken with regard to the course of this process of change, especially because he presumed that the transformation would take the form of political revolutions of the bourgeois-democratic type. He saw the world revolution in proletarian and Europe-centered terms and did not foresee the rise of the totalitarian states that turn man and his transformation into objects to be manipulated by élites. In actual fact the European working class did not become a passive victim of the economic trend to absolute or relative pauperization—a trend which did exist in Marx's time—and so it had neither the reason nor the objective possibility to overthrow the ruling classes in those most advanced capitalist countries in which Marx expected the world revolution to begin. Marx was not wrong about the basic trend of social evolution, nor in his vision of future society, but he was mistaken when, being too strongly influenced by his own age, he assumed that the basic trends of the nineteenth century would continue, as is especially apparent in his theory of the absolute pauperization of the working class.

28. The most significant factor in the transformation of the human scene and in the changed relations between the individual and society is the totalitarian state. This is a realization of the idea that people are to be managed by bureaucracy and that human freedom is to be subordinated to other values, to the state, the nation, the party, the class, God, the personality of the leader. The perfect totalitarian state is an integral system, a power structure distinguished by at least three features: (1) the monopoly of absolute, uncontrollable power; (2) the continuity of the system, whereby all vacancies among the élite are filled from within the élite's own ranks (not by election); (3) the reign of fear, because the polarization into the absolute power of the élites and the absolute powerlessness of the masses makes both sides feel permanently threatened; (4) the official status of the lie guaranteed by a binding ideology, which justifies facts regardless

of whether they make sense or not, but always on the basis of their effect on the stability of the élite's power, that is, their purely functional aspect; (5) the reduction of man to a fragment that can be used in the totalitarian system of apparatuses of manipulation; for the system cannot use man as a free being, but only as a fragment of the mass.

29. Several of these features of totalitarianism are present to some extent in all the industrial societies of today; in the fascist states they all existed at the same time and in a heightened form. These features of the totalitarian state are determined by the mass society, mass production and consumption of industrial goods and by the permanent arms race, while the central question of our time is precisely whether humanity, the societies and their élites will be able to control these trends or not. Thus we are faced with the question: Can man be free in the age of totalitarian systems? The question is at once an invitation and a guideline to the defense of freedom under entirely new and unusual circumstances. First of all, we are not following any ideological fetishes (not even the fetish of freedom) and so we must not allow ourselves to be taken in by ideologies, which would like to persuade us that the solution lies in moving from one ideology to another, from Marxism to liberalism or Thomism or vice versa. We are not concerned with changes in ideology—whether at the moment they happen to be following a tougher or a more liberal line—but with the real transformations in the world of manipulated objects, with the transmutations of human existence.

30. We must therefore realize that we are living in a qualitatively new society, which openly tends toward totalitarianism, while at the same time we must not measure this society either against the past democratic ideology or against a utopian projection into the future. What is important for us is not how this society judges itself, whether it sees itself as good or bad, or what it calls itself, whether Communist or democratic, but of what kind this society actually *is*, what is its new élite, what are its social stratifications and cultural differentiation, its scales of values, which today openly differ at different social levels. We

have no reason to insist upon the folkloristic peculiarities of Czechoslovak socialism or upon ideological camouflages, but we must be deeply concerned with the real changes in the very structures of this society, because we are imprisoned in it, and that for life—not by the stretches of ploughed-up land along our frontiers, but by our own history.

Conclusion

31. Broadly speaking we can say that the basic trend of modern society is the growing scope of manipulation, using technological means to control not only production and labor, but also man and his history. In this sense Hans Freyer speaks about the following converging trends: it is becoming increasingly feasible to produce things, to control labor, to civilize man and to control history—"Machbarkeit der Sachen, Organisierbarkeit der Arbeit, Zivilisierbarkeit des Menschen, Volendbarkeit der Geschichte" (*Theorie des gegenwärtigen Zeitalters*, Stuttgart, 1955). Today we might add these further trends: entertainment and leisure are becoming more and more mechanized and sexual life more and more "democratized." Human freedom is more gravely threatened by these objective trends of social evolution than it has ever been before, because they are conspiring together against man and against the humanist tradition.

32. These evolutionary trends are now asserting themselves in the midst of the conflict between the élites which represent the world power blocs and are striving for world hegemony. Although these élites' ideologies claim that they are concerned with the liberation of the oppressed (always, of course, oppressed by the rival bloc), what is really at issue is the seizing of power by the apparatuses of the totalitarian states and the securing of economic or political influence in the third world. Meanwhile the competition of monopoly capitalism and state capitalism is presented ideologically as a fight to defend the freedom of man (against the opposite side), though it is purely the struggle of

managerial groups for the organization of the world and for power. The world is controlled by the supermanagers of giant economic, political and power mechanisms, to whom humanist aims mean nothing. The tendency to manipulation extends beyond the totalitarian states and nations in the form of the threat of war and of world disaster.

33. Man living under the pressure of totalitarianism, manipulation and nuclear war is becoming more and more conditioned to the transformation of the social scene, until he comes to consider it as the normal and natural environment of his life. Provided that the state is not ruled by a murdering paranoiac but by a group striving for the rational organization of society, the mass man sees the satisfaction of his needs as a counterpart to the élite's claim to government and he has no reason to concern himself with the abstract problem of freedom. He does not feel the manipulation, except possibly as a good thing. If, on the other hand, he protests, he willy-nilly finds himself either in isolation or taking a heroic attitude, because the defense of the human personality, of man's freedom, appears to the manipulated, smiling and consuming robots as sheer quixotry.

34. The intellectuals who are willing to find their bearings in this way among the ideological blackmail and the power struggles of the managerial élites are the latent or open enemies of the totalitarian state and they are therefore rightly considered to be dangerous. The degree to which the administrative apparatuses are aggressive toward the intellectuals accurately reflects the degree to which they feel insecure. An expansion of absurdity always begins with a pogrom of intellects. At present, it is not expedient or effective or possible for an individual to oppose the apparatus openly, as a matter of principle, if the opposition is to take the form of practical action. But it is possible, necessary and effective in the sphere of thought.

The Meaning of
Marxism

[1966]

Master Chuang was walking with Master Huey on the bridge
over the river Hao. Master Chuang said, "See how free and gay
the fish are as they swim below the surface. That is what fish
like best!" Master Huey answered, "But you are not a fish. How
can you know what the fish like?" "And you are not me, so how
can you know that I do not know what fish like?" "I am not
you, so it is true that I cannot know what you know, but it is
just as true that you are not a fish, and that proves that you do
not know what fish like!" Master Chuang said, "Let us return to
where we begun. You said, how can I know what fish like? Whoever asked this, must have asked already knowing that I do know.
And I did know it, when we were above the river Hao."

—CHUANG-TZU, old Chinese philosopher

Philosophical Assumptions

1. Hermeneutics, the art of interpreting the text from its context, assumes that the meaning of the text can be derived from
the text alone. It presupposes that the meaning of the text is
homogeneous and sees the system it analyzes as a closed, logically
indivisible whole. Such an interpretation of Marxist texts would
be wrong *a priori*, quite apart from the fact that today even the
most extreme exponents of Maoism no longer defend so academic
and dogmatic a conception of Marxism.

2. A modern interpretation of Karl Marx's texts must bear in mind the historical, sociological and philosophical context of the work it is interpreting. So it takes into account the historical development of Marxism, the sociological structure of the societies that gradually transformed the meaning of the movement, and the changes in the philosophical approach to the aims of socialism.

3. Materialist dialectics regards every system that it analyzes as open, liable to be affected by historical and social evolution. Therefore it requires that the changes in the meaning and aims of the doctrine it is analyzing be recognized. These shifts of meaning cannot be considered as a "betrayal of principles" but as the necessary concomitant of the development of ideology, of learning or of a given work. The original meaning of philosophical or moral ideas and their function in the historical process may move far apart.

4. Consequently, materialist dialectics must consider Marxism, too, as a changing ideology, the meaning of which is being transformed in the course of time. It rejects the idea that the original texts have a timeless and absolute validity, and therefore its approach is determined not by an analysis of the texts alone but rather by the confrontation of the texts with their historical background, with the structure of society and with class interests. According to the Marxist classics, Marxism must change even with new discoveries in natural science.

5. In regarding the system we are analyzing—for instance, Marxism—as a historically changing, open structure, we do not necessarily deny that the central texts and principles remain relatively stable. The transformations and shifts in the meaning of the text under the effect of new historical experience and the evolution of knowledge concern rather the secondary issues, while the central principles endure. But then the question arises, which principles are central and which are not, the question of the hierarchy of aims and values in the given system and of the authenticity of any one interpretation; we may also wonder which interpretation is to be considered as authoritative and who is to have the right to provide this standard interpretation.

6. In the solution of these problems in Marxism, the criterion of actual practice must play an exceptionally large role; principles must be checked against the way they are applied in the labor movement or in state politics. But if the interpretation of Marxism is bound up with the different practices of Communist parties under various historical and social conditions, then a diversity of interpretations, varying with the identity and interests of the interpreter, must also be admitted. The multiplicity of interpretations raises the problem of deciding which one is "objectively true" and who has the right to provide the standard interpretation, and creates the need to tolerate differences of opinion within certain limits and, on the other hand, to enforce solidarity with the authoritative decisions.

7. The variety in the interpretation of the aims and meaning of Marx's teaching, which is unwelcome but follows from the variety of actual practice, leads to constant internal divisions, to the rise of deviations and the struggle against them, so that the history of Marxism can be—and during the Stalin era was—conceived as the history of deviations and the fight of orthodoxy against heresy. Several interpretations of Marxism always exist side by side and are closely interrelated, while each of the different variants claims that its version of the ideology and of the movement is the only true one. This gives rise to ideological conflicts, which are, however, only a cover for the power struggle between the European and the Asian-Byzantine tendencies of socialism.

8. In this way Marx's teaching is perverted from its original form into an ideology, a false understanding of reality, while the objective analysis of social problems is repressed in favor of expedient, schematic apologetics. But ideologies—thanks precisely to Marx himself—have long been recognized as the camouflage of vested interests, as syntheses of self-deceptions and illusions; so the transformation of the meaning of Marxism holds no mystery for us if we understand the power structures and the social forces that have imposed on Marxism its present-day form.

9. Insofar as Marxism itself has become an ideology, it must be

dealt with according to Marx's own criteria, which follow from the philosophical principles of dialectical materialism: all interpretations are historically determined; the meaning of the texts is relatively changeable; the central texts and principal objectives of socialism are relatively stable; the real criterion is actual practice; many interpretations are possible; self-deception must be unmasked and the power struggle that underlies the conflict of ideas, exposed.

10. The conflict of ideological tendencies in Marxism then appears as the conflict of power blocs over the right to provide the standard interpretation and as a screen of ideas used to mask the power struggle for world domination, which is hostile to humanism in all its forms. The conflict between the Byzantine and the Asian orientations merely hides the conflict between the European and the non-European, the scientific and the ideological, the humanist and the authoritarian conceptions of socialism and of Marx's heritage.

Historical Transformations of Marxism

11. The central texts of Marxism may be said to be those which determine the basic aim of socialism in the conception of Karl Marx. Philosophical historiography can show, by objective methods and independently of any ideological leanings, that the aims which Marx associated with socialism (communism) were an extension of nineteenth-century European culture and of the radical humanism deriving from the European tradition of antiquity, the Renaissance and the Enlightenment. The founders of Marxism attributed to socialism at least three principal aims: (1) a broader freedom for individual people and the development of their human potentialities; (2) the transformation of social relations, especially ownership, which was expressed at the time as a demand for a social and not merely a political revolution; (3) the emancipation of the working class as the chief historical bearer of revolutionary change.

12. Marx strove for the transformation of man and his place in society so that he might play a new role in history; he did not strive for state power, nor for totalitarian manipulation, nor for world domination by Communism. Power and the state were to be only a temporary means to the end and were soon to wither away. These aims, which even the enemies of Marxism must recognize were demonstrably and indisputably the goals the founders had in view, provide a yardstick which can be used to determine whether the various current ideological variants of Marxism are pursuing Marx's real goals or not. On the other hand, the criterion cannot lie in pragmatically conceived power politics, authoritarian decision-making or a faith in fictitious values or economicomilitary successes.

13. As regards this central meaning of Marxism, we can say that five principal solutions to the problem of authority and interpretation, all strikingly different from one another, were successively evolved in the course of time. They appeared historically as different kinds of Marxism. The relation between authority and interpretation took different forms according to who was interpreting the aims of Marxist socialism, whether it was Karl Marx, the labor movement, the revolutionary party, the party apparatus or, finally, a given leader.

14. In the first historical stage of revolutionary Marxism there appeared to be no problem of authority, because Marx himself interpreted the aims of his own teaching and at the same time headed the International as the acknowledged leader of the movement. His idea of socialism grew up in the conflicts with non-Marxist socialism (Proudhon, Bakunin, Lassalle), the social revolution seemed to be near and the movement itself was seen as democratic. But it will not escape the attention of anyone closely familiar with Marx's development that in this first stage of revolutionary Marxism there arose, within Marx's work itself, two basic variants of his conception of the meaning of socialism (communism), which were only much later discovered as the version of "the young Marx" and that of "the Marx of the *Capital*". In other words, Marx's work itself already provides two basic inter-

pretations of his own work, the humanist version and the economic version.

15. In the social-democratic tradition of an evolutionary conception of Marxism, it is the activity of the working class itself which has the authority to provide the standard interpretation. So the idea which arose at the time, that "the movement is all," that the mass movement is in itself the final arbiter of truth, was quite consistent. The meaning and goal of socialism were being created by the spontaneous action of the labor movement, and both E. Bernstein and Rosa Luxemburg, as well as Trotsky, though they differed in their attitude toward the revolution, considered the acting masses to be the authentic interpreters of socialism.

16. Leninism represented a radical departure from these trends in the way it applied Marxism to the conditions in Russia, stressing in its program the role of the political party and attributing to it, rather than to the movement itself, the decisive role in the leadership. This *ipso facto* incited the party to claim for itself the sole right to expound socialism and the paths toward it, a monopoly which, for the time being, was effective only superficially, since in the then conditions of the social-democratic (later communist) parties, it could not be enforced by the authority of state power. Martov, Plekhanov, Trotsky and Rosa Luxemburg criticized as narrowly Russian, un-European and undemocratic Lenin's idea that the political party is the guardian of the labor movement. It was no longer the labor movement itself but its representatives and the political party that gave socialism its meaning. Before he died, Lenin became aware of the problem inherent in this narrow and specifically Russian conception of Marxism and of the political party.

17. Since the meaning and the development of socialism were no longer determined by the labor movement itself, it was only logical that after Lenin's death the representatives of the party asserted even more firmly their exclusive right to interpret socialism. The Stalinist deformation narrowed the party's monopoly still further, restricting it to the party apparatus. This apparatus,

together with the direct executive power, enforced more and more ruthlessly its authority to make decisions, and physically eliminated all potential or actual opponents. As in the Byzantine tradition of the relations between the church and state, the party and the state now became one. The aims of Marxism as the revolutionary class movement of the workers were sacrificed to the interests of the state, and the elucidation of the theoretical objectives of socialism was subordinated to the interests of the power state and of Russian nationalism.

18. Stalinism brought about a decisive change, in that first the apparatus and then the top of the apparatus created, seized and enforced their monopoly to interpret Marxism. From that time on, the aims of socialism were determined purely pragmatically, in relation to the immediate situation of the soviet state. Principles became puppets to be freely manipulated in the interests of power. This tendency is even more pronounced in Maoism, not only because the supreme interpreter is the leader of the movement and of the state, but also because the means that can be used to attain the end include nuclear war.

19. The evolutionary stages of the ramification, subdivision and differentiation of Marx's original teaching suggest several conclusions about the relation between interpretation and authority: (1) the circle of interpreters has grown steadily narrower and the interpretation itself has been subjected to procedures which have turned it into the privileged activity of the power holders. (2) The humanist-democratic interpretation of Marxism, corresponding to the original sense of Marx's teaching, has been pushed further and further into the background by the pragmatic-economic conception, in which the socialist emancipation of man degenerates into an economic program for a mature industrial society. (3) Under the Stalinist regime of personal dictatorship and violation of basic human rights, the fundamental aims of the movement were openly denied and radically transformed. Marxism became the totalitarian ideology of the soviet state and openly broke away from the European humanist tradition.

20. The aims of Marxist socialism (communism) are today

determined, not only politically but also ideologically, on the basis that the goal of the socialist movement is an efficient economy, the accurate manipulation of the mechanisms of power and a high rate of consumption, not the humanist program of remolding man and society in order to attain greater freedom. These tendencies deny the original ideas of Karl Marx and destroy the meaning of the social transformations of the proletarian revolution. The authority of power has forcibly deprived the rank-and-file supporters of socialism of their rightful share in deciding and interpreting the aims of the movement. The manipulation of ideological formulas by the bureaucratic apparatuses of the power élites has replaced critical thought and thus created a situation in which Marxism can be fruitfully discussed only outside the apparatus's sphere of influence. The effort by Marxist theory and practice to overcome this state of affairs is meeting enormous obstacles. Why?

The Structures of Society and the Transformations of Ideology

21. The changes in the way Marx's teaching is interpreted cannot be explained only by reference to personalities, to political events or to the inner dialectic of the labor movement. The marked tendency to move away from the democratic activity of the broad masses to the administrative control of the masses by power apparatuses is an expression of structural changes in the industrial societies of both East and West. These new social structures affect social awareness, the aims and values of socialism and even the forms of thought themselves.

22. Social structures play an essential part in the shaping of society's conception of itself, its utopian-ideological or scientifically objective process of learning, the formation of its self-awareness and self-deceptions. This happens through mechanisms which are approximately known to the sociology of knowledge. The most important factors are the interests of classes and power élites, the relationship between the ruling ideology and state

power, and the character of state power in the cultural tradition of the society.

23. The central issue is the relation between the ruling ideology and the institutions of power, more specifically, the relationship of socialist ideology to state power. Marxist ideology has played three distinct roles in relation to the state: (1) it was a criticism of capitalism and took a negative stand on state power; (2) while revolutionary forces were being built up, and in the transitional period, it was an ideology defending state power and at the same time criticizing the state, with the aim of bringing about its disappearance; (3) in the socialist states it has become a mere apologetic for the given conditions, it has lost its critical function and turned into a means of defending the interests of the power élite.

24. In the beginnings of Marxism, the socialist movement acquired a democratic character under the influence of the democratic structure of West European capitalist countries. The fact that this movement was in opposition and had no means of obtaining the instruments of power ensured its internal democracy, so that Marxism was rightly regarded as a consistent form of democracy and the culmination of the freedom and human rights of the bourgeois democracies. The creation of the state power of the Soviet Union, in the dramatic circumstances when socialism was isolated inside a single country, gave the party apparatus an increasing influence on the formation of the ideology and its aims. The activity of broad sectors of society, and of the working class, was essentially replaced by the self-seeking of the apparent spokesmen of the working class—the power élite. But state power was still seen as an instrument of world revolution and of the emancipation of mankind.

25. Under Stalinism, the function of the soviet state was conceived without reference to the original humanist aims of socialist ideology. The transformation of the meaning of Marxism reached its culminating point when the structure of the totalitarian state came to be reflected in its ideology, in the forms of social consciousness. The exclusion of people's democratic participation in

government, the police control of thought, the abolition of fundamental human rights and the harsh repression of real or apparent deviations, including the physical elimination of opponents, made all dialogue impossible. Marxist theory is only now beginning to make a positive effort, in the form of "revisionist" thought as against the "dogmatism" of the Stalin era, to return to the original sources of Marx and Lenin. These tendencies are most evident in the Communist parties of the Western countries, where the party apparatus does not have the administrative power to forbid such thinking. Similar tendencies are being tacitly tolerated in the countries of the socialist camp in certain spheres of philosophy and art, provided they are so remote from the interests of the power élite that it does not feel threatened by them.

26. The attempts to win the recognition and observance of basic human rights in the face of the state's monopoly of power to regulate thought are provoking strong opposition in the apparatuses. Differences of opinion in the conception of socialist aims may be *de facto* admitted in the international Communist movement, but in principle they are still unacceptable and seen as a threat to the role of the apparatus within the Communist parties. Some of these parties maintain principles of organization that do not admit the discussion of fundamental issues even within the party or the state, because the apparatuses rightly see that all discussion represents a threat to the power they wield as an uncontrolled élite. Dialogue is replaced by duets of manipulated monologues. The present compromise of apparent toleration of national differences and insistence on conformity within the parties is an indication of the uncertainty surrounding the final aims of socialism and the ways of achieving them.

27. Striking differences in the interpretation of the aims and meaning of socialism appear in the thinking of both Eastern and Western Communists as well as among the individual countries of the socalist camp. In those countries where the apparatus does not hold state power, these differences can be explained by the differences in the social regimes of these countries. But a similar variety in conceptions of socialism also exists in the different

social layers of one country and of one Communist party, although it is not publicly expressed. The interpretation and understanding of socialism differs according to membership of a given social class, that is, whether one belongs to the working class, to the middle class or to the power élite. At the same time the cultural tradition, the masses' educational level and the country's technological maturity also leave their mark on the interpretation of Marxism. So one can say that, even in the toughest period of Stalinism in the fifties, the East European countries did not adopt the soviet model of state power and state ideology in its entirety; they were prevented from doing so by the fact that they had had a higher level of culture and broader civil rights than had been common under Czarism.

28. The changes that occurred in the aims of Marxist ideology in relation to the changing character of state power show that the structures of power in a given society are reflected in the way the aims of Marxism are conceived. But the fundamental change that lies in the return to the humanist aims of Marxism cannot be brought about by the simple adoption of humanist phraseology, which yesterday's Stalinists are now tolerating and even encouraging. This radical change can be achieved only by a transformation of the structural relations between power and ideology, between the masses and the parties, between the activity of the people and a bureaucratic administration, in other words, only by a democratization that accepts freedom of opinion and variety in the interpretations of Marxism.

29. The hierarchical structure of Soviet society in the Stalin era was reflected in ideology as an interpretation of the classical texts in legal and police terms. Stalin's truth was a degradation of Lenin's, Lenin's truth was a degradation of Marx. It was on this basis alone that it became possible to impose a *concordantia discordantium canonum*, and then only as an act of police censorship, not because the system had any inner consistency. Expediency replaced truth, and manipulation of these was substituted for the spirit of learning. Marxism thus temporarily became an incoherent, pragmatic jumble, composed of unrelated precepts that could be reshuffled at will.

30. The transformation of the post-Stalin Soviet Union into a technologically mature industrial society may have brought with it increasing prosperity and military strength; but at the same time this society adopted a modified version of the American way of life and set a high rate of consumption as its primary objective. For the time being, the economic interpretation of the aims of socialism predominates over the conceptions that link socialism with humanism; but although the administrations are trying to suppress them, it still looks as if these conceptions have a bright future before them. For Marxists who understand the logic of the evolution of the soviet state and its ideology, it seems inevitable that there will come a further polarization, which will either renew the methods of Stalinism and so come closer to Maoism, or Marxism will again adopt the European values of Marx's humanism and find a new acceptance in Europe and in the world.

The Sources of Socialist Humanism

[1963]

"Where have we come from? Who are we? Where are we going?" These three simple questions were the title of a painting by an artist who, at the close of the last century, left Europe—not because he preferred the empty idyll of the Tahitian islands, but because he wanted to seek the attitudes of life that, by the primitiveness of the questions they posed, could give rise to endless paraphrases of the key problem of the meaning of life. Thus the artist Paul Gauguin, with no philosophical, religious, or scientific ambitions, expressed the very questions that may be considered the main problem of all the religions of the world and the basic concept of all past philosophies of man, as well as the central content of every humanism.

Who is man? The answer to Gauguin's simple question is very difficult and at the same time very important. The most general instruments of human thinking, i.e., categories, cannot really be scientifically defined, precisely because they are categories, or very general notions. They are so basic and fundamental that they are subordinate only to the concept of being, so that a true definition could state only that categories exist. That in itself would have no meaning, and as a definition it would be absurd. The same can be said of man, not only because he is the category of all categories, but because he himself is their creator. He is on both ends of the definition at the same time: he is both *definiens* and *definiendum*. If we nevertheless wish to define man, the best way to do so is by his history. *Man is a history of his own definitions, the determination of himself.* So far, the number of definitions that have been put forward throughout the history and the development of man's understanding of himself are, to a certain extent, in accord with the history of social formations. The image man has created of himself has varied, because man has reflected the world and himself in the world in various ways, depending upon the social relationships he has had. Although biologically *Homo sapiens* has remained the same, his consciousness of himself and his self-understanding have changed with his changing social organization. Man's monumental self-portraits, and his understanding of the historical process of his own development of thinking, are still, to a certain extent, the live nucleus of mass ideologies and the basic concept which animates both such ideologies and the arts, religion, and philosophy. *Homo peccator*, the essential concept of Christianity; *Homo faber*, the center of liberal doctrine; and the Socialist vision of nonalienated, total man—these are various answers to the ancient question of human meaning.

A knowledge of the various answers to the question of man—those currently given by the East and the West, as well as the traditional Christian, liberal, and socialist answers—is a prerequisite of mutual understanding. In the dialogue of ideologies, where reproaches for the absence of humanism are often heard, it is important to remember that Marxism stems from the same classical sources of eighteenth- and nineteenth-century European humanism as non-Marxist and nonsocialist traditions. An understanding of this *common* source and link between different humanist ideologies—an understanding of man as the central value of history—has become more important today than the study of the differences among the various types of humanism.

Socialist humanism did not develop by the blind mechanism of economic history, but by solving the "eternal" questions of man and his significance in the universe. In spite of the fact that man's development may seem preordained by the solution of the social problems of industrial society, this is in fact an illusion. Reducing the socialist movement and its concept of man to the realization of social reform and revolution means passing over an important dimension of socialism—its humanistic aim. The birth of socialist thought was the result of the development of European humanism, a tradition that has its deepest roots in ancient Greece, the Renaissance, and the Enlightenment.

The Prologue to Marxist Humanism

For many centuries of the Christian era the concept of man was dominated by the idea of the dualism of body and soul. Anthropology was a theological discipline primarily concerned with the relationship of man to God, although the amount of knowledge about the soul was far less than the available knowledge about the human body. Then, in the nineteenth century, came Ludwig Feuerbach. Preserving the secular concept of the Renaissance and the Enlightenment, Feuerbach reversed the theological point of view and proclaimed that man was God, thus becoming one of the discoverers of modern man.

Feuerbach's anthropology, a universal science of man, was the peak of pre-Marxist humanism. It represents a historical development where philosophical knowledge arrived at a formulation of the scope and aim of the study of the human race—a theory of man. Feuerbach's materialistic concept was in sharp contradiction to the spiritualistic Christian concept, because its point of departure was not an abstract *notion* of man, but *concrete man*. Speculative philosophy put the essence of man outside himself; Hegel's system even placed thinking outside man, and made it a special nonhuman substance. Against this philosophy, which alienates man from his essence, Feuerbach saw man as a sensual being and sketched a grandiose concept of a dialectical triad in which primitive man, living in harmony with his natural essence, goes through religious alienation and becomes a victim of his own projection until the necessity to return to himself brings his reintegration.

In Feuerbach's case, philosophical humanism did not use speculation—as it had during most of its history—but rather a union with the knowledge acquired by the natural sciences. Man, said Feuerbach, should be understood as an entity, not as a thinking ego; he should become a personalized, practical, active agent. Where previous systems had always fused the ego with some act of intellectual consciousness, Feuerbach liberated concrete man in all his reality, not only in his thinking. And in this "real humanism" lay the basic theoretical position of later Marxism and socialism.

In Feuerbach's system elements of "vulgar" materialism blend with a deep philosophical understanding of man; a vague anticipation of socialism as human solidarity is joined with the utopian solution of the renaissance of man through love; a mystic relationship between the man-God and his fellowmen is linked with an objective, realistic understanding of the importance of concrete human relationships. The indistinct vision of love and the communion of human hearts is the starting point of a road leading to a scientific understanding of man. The conclusion of Feuerbach's *Principles of the Philosophy of the Future* proclaims the necessity of abandoning speculation completely, and this is the beginning of the future humanism of Karl Marx. The whole of man—the total thinking, feeling, loving man—becomes the subject of the new philosophy and of atheistic, humanistic anthropology.

Feuerbach's concept broke through not only Hegelian but all other abstractions, and its importance is multiplied when we realize that in Feuerbach love is a transformed Christian love of one's neighbor. For Feuerbach love is not only sensual bliss but also the very definition of man's social belonging, an expression of his substance, of his unity with other men. Love is human naturalness, an affirmation of man's humanness. Feuerbach's man always exists in a dialectical unity of "I and Thou," or, to be more exact, man himself is "I and Thou." *Man is defined as a relationship.* For the first time in the history of philosophical anthropology man is recognized as a constantly *changing relationship.* *I* is firmly anchored in *Thou.* The concrete human relations that Feuerbach's philosophy introduced to us are not so fruitful as Marx's later concept of man as the whole sum of social relations. But they nevertheless lay the foundation for this concept.

Feuerbach transformed love into a concrete human category, and made it an important aspect of his total man. But, despite his efforts toward a concrete concept, he remained the prisoner of an abstract cult of man, unable to explain him in *all* his social aspects. In the narrow concept of I and Thou, he understood man quite concretely in the field of sexual and family relations. However, this was the only truly concrete aspect he was able to capture. Man as a whole remained a kind of vague, deified man-God. And when the historical process, striving toward a socialist society, replaced the utopian way of achieving love among people, Feuerbach's theories gave way to the revolutionary practice of the people themselves. The theoretical expression of this further phase of humanism was a historical, materialistic, and dialectical understanding of man and his role in the transformation of the world.

Fundamentals of Marxist Humanism

This new kind of humanism was formulated for the first time in Paris, in the spring of 1844, by a twenty-six-year-old immigrant from Germany named Karl Marx. His unfinished manuscript had one of the most dramatic fates of any book. Even today any reference to Marx's *Economic and Philosophic Manuscripts of 1844* arouses the interest of both orthodox and unorthodox Marxists. The gist of this work can be expressed as follows: *Communism without humanism is no communism and humanism without communism cannot be humanism.* From the maze of the Hegelian and Feuerbachian prose in which Marx then wrote, at least three important concepts of man emerge, which form the basis of Marxian humanism. Together they comprise a historical triad of the human race's dramatic process of development, from the state of a natural identity through its social development to its own freedom; from the alienation of its humane basis through the overcoming of alienation to the goal of history—communism; from nature through inhumaneness to humaneness. The grand contours of the picture Marx painted of man's self-understanding and self-realization rise above anything that the theories of the Enlightenment created, either in its French mechanistic-materialistic branch, or in its German, Hegelian idealistic branch. Marx transcends the limits of bourgeois society within which even the most radical bourgeois democratic ideology had until then remained. The concept of man as a separate individual was surpassed.

To give a complete picture of Marx's understanding of anthropology, one must refer to his later works. Limiting the Marxist philosophy of man to the works of the *young* Marx would misrepresent Marx's humanism. Since Landshut has tried to introduce ethics into anthropology, anti-Marxist critics have "theologized" Marx's concept of man. They have misinterpreted the meaning of man's path from primeval freedom through alienation to future freedom as the fall of man, his penitence, and salvation. But any interpretation of Marx which is not in accord with the spirit of contemporary science is not correct, whether it be an ideological concept of ethical socialism, theology, revisionism, or orthodox dogmatism. And, at the same time, any concept that would exclude from communism the humanistic basis of the young Marx, be it in favor of the mechanics of economic forces, the class struggle, the interest of the ruling class, or power of the contemporary state, is an antihumanist and anti-Marxist concept, regardless of the phraseology used.

Marx's picture of man, compared to earlier philosophical ideas, differs qualitatively, especially in the concept of man as an active subject, his own creator, who struggles with forms of alienation and consummates himself. This radical change must be stressed, without denying that the existentialist branch of philosophical thinking has formed yet another concept of man. Marx's dialectical anthropology is not final, because knowledge, which becomes part of science, is subject to the criticism of time, and because the further development of science transcends it. The works of Marx are thus not the end of the history of anthropology and humanism, but a turning point, after which anthropological typology continues. The most important mark of dialectical anthropology is the constant broadening of the concept of man, as the model becomes more and more complicated. The cycle of change in the concept of man that has taken place in philosophy during the last six thousand years continues as an exponential curve beyond Marx himself. One can picture the growth of scientific knowledge about man as a quickly rising curve, climbing to the open future, like man himself.

Marx's concept of humanism brought a basic change into the history of humanism, since it was more than the mere metaphysical speculation of the German philosophy of the time. It transcended older philosophies and formed an anti-illusionist, anti-ideological social and historical basis for scientific anthropology. Among other things, it *brought to a close the old philosophy of man by laying the basis for a science of man.*

Marx formulated the prerequisites of humanism, founded on a *scientific* anthropology. One hundred years after Marx, there are, of course, a number of specific branches of science which either did not exist in the second half of the last century or were of negligible importance. Scientific anthropology and humanism have a new empirical basis, although the ideas and concepts of Marx's theory have not lost their validity. As the discoverer of the real mechanism of human alienation, Marx is basically in accord with contemporary science—with the understanding of man as a process, an open system, a flowing equilibrium. Modern science is filling in the contours of man sketched by the young and versatile genius with dialectical concreteness during a Paris spring. Marxist philosophy is an organic product of European culture and of a European, that is to say, classical and humanist, concept of man. If Marxist philosophy is now to begin to formulate the socialist-humanist concept of man and to expound the ideas contained in Marx's manuscripts, it must do this in accordance not only with the classical heritage of the pre-Marxist concept of man, but with that of contemporary science. Marxist philosophers are aware of the fact that they have yet to formulate a more detailed answer to the question, "Who is man?" than the broad contours formulated one hundred and twenty years ago by a young German philosopher.

Scientific Anthropology as the Basis of Socialist Humanism

In recent years, problems of theoretical humanism have been neglected and deformed in Marxist philosophy by the personality cult. The achievements of contemporary social science have not been sufficiently absorbed by the philosophy of dialectical materialism. The work of Roger Garaudy, Adam Schaff, and Karel Kosík in evaluating contemporary philosophical anthropology and existentialism is an important step forward in the whole approach to the problem, but these authors themselves do not consider their conclusions definite. Marxist historiography has not yet come to grips with the works of Kierkegaard, Husserl, and Scheler.

With the enormous specialization that has taken place in the natural sciences during the last hundred years, the amassed knowledge concerning man has come to form several separate branches of science. Besides philosophical anthropologies, of which there are a number, at least eight special branches of anthropology come into existence that deal with the realities of man by *scientific* methods as well as by philosophical reflection. If there is a point of departure in humanism that follows Karl Marx, it is the attempt to draw conclusions about man on a firmer basis than philosophical reasonings offer, in short, on the basis of science. Marx's contribution was to show how barren were the pretensions of any metaphysics aspiring to capture the world in its totality and express its entirety; he proved that from a scientific point of view man cannot be described effectively by any *philosophical* anthropology; he must be subjected to the analytical scalpel of the scientific method, which can disclose the biological, psychological, historical, and social tissues of human existence, and give philosophy the material for forming a synthesis. In the twentieth century, humanism must be supplemented by the scientific analysis of man.

Insofar as the main branches of science have produced a great amount of knowledge about man, we may speak of physical, biological, psychological, sociological, cultural, prehistoric, economic and ethnographic anthropology, each of which answers the question of who man is through specialized methods. Without trespassing beyond their own methodology, these sciences treat the origin of man, his specifications in comparison to animals, his personality as the creator of culture, his history, social relationships, ecology, economic possibilities, etc. Single problems have been worked out to various degrees; some remain long-range tasks for a future anthropological synthesis, while for others there is already elaborate and to some extent generalized material. Biological, historical, sociological and psychological data make it possible to issue the most important results of contemporary knowledge about man as a *synthetic science*—anthropology—and to form a sufficiently large fund of knowledge for modern humanism and philosophical theory to draw upon.

In the field of contemporary biology, entirely new knowledge has come to light: man has been shown to be an open, unspecialized entity, the product of a specific rhythm of growth (as described by A. Portmann), which is unique in the development of life and achieves a very special standing in the animal world. Biology has proved that man's first year of life is an extremely important phase of his growth, similar to what in other mammals takes place during the development of the embyro inside the womb, and that the period of acquiring knowledge, which is exceptionally long in man, produces a peculiar rhythm of life in regard to sexual maturity and the cycle of reproduction—all of which suggests that man's distinction from animals has biological foundations.

Similarly, revolutionary information on man has been contributed by modern psychology, which in both its branches, the

Pavlovian and the Freudian, has substantially changed the previously held image of man as a reasoning individual by showing that many forces besides consciousness govern him. Whatever the terminology, the psychologists' image of man is always of an entity of many layers, of which reason is not the most important. Man is seen as constantly changing, and all the manifold roles through which the individual passes in his development are taken into account. The psychology of the personality, together with social psychology, delves into the structure of human nature and at the same time provides a great many empirical facts.

After biology and psychology, sociology has achieved the most important new understanding of man. Aristotle's words about the society of man were given a new content when Marx approached man as a set of not only personal but social relations. At the same time, the concept of man as a member of a collective class—a nation, family, or larger or smaller social group—has made it possible to understand the social aspect of human existence and the growing importance of groups in the life of modern man. Whole social classes have accepted the revolutionary idea that a change in man requires a change in the given social relationships; that a program of changing the world is in accord with the evolution of society. Man is discovering himself as the conscious creator of social relationships and, thanks to Marx and Freud, now knows that, because of alienation, he has been a mere plaything in the hands of forces which he did not understand. This fuller knowledge of man has not remained the privilege of a few, but has become the theory of living, human, transforming practice. Man knows now that to "think means to change," as Bertolt Brecht so aptly put it.

Scientific anthropology is beginning to formulate its first answers to the problem of human existence, with due acknowledgment to past thinkers. Man is an open entity, a personality, and the sum of his relationships. He originated in nature, in history, in the development of societies and cultures; he is going forth to a humane world, toward the mastery of technology, the creation and the metamorphosis of man in time. "Where have we come from? Who are we? Where are we going?" We come from history; we are people; we are going forth to meet ourselves. These are the prolegomena of scientific anthropology to socialist humanism, to the philosophy of man, to the philosophy of man's freedom.

The Future of Humanism

It is, of course, impossible to reduce socialist humanism to the empirical data of the sciences, because it is also concerned with the problem of values and a vision of the future of mankind, which goes beyond science.

Pierre Lecomte du Noüy tells us that the future of man is the only transcendentalism left to materialists who deny God. We agree that the question of the future of mankind is indeed one of the most important. Religious thinkers have been convinced that the history of personalities, nations and the whole of mankind was in some manner predestined. The question of the goal of history or the future of man was thus senseless, because history was a revelation of God's aims. In the later years of the Enlightenment an uncritical belief in the progress of mankind was prevalent, but the people of the twentieth century have reached beyond this belief, only to strive the harder for their own rational futures as the sole alternative to total destruction. The world of tomorrow is a modern world without war, a world of mutual enrichment of cultures. The future of mankind will be conditioned by the mastery of technology, economic growth, automation of production and an invasion of the sciences into the everyday life of man, which will perhaps free man for creation and thus change his way of life. This perspective of economic affluence and a society without classes presents a vision whose contours are lost to the scientist in the space of the cosmos and the depth of time, where science remains silent and the philosopher and poet have their say.

This is where true philosophy begins, because here begins an area of reasoning that empirical science cannot encompass. Here scientific anthropology is transformed into active and concrete humanism, into practical human activity, which is leading the world in the direction of socialism. But the essence of socialism is not the growth of material wealth; it is the full development of man and his liberation. The older utopians as well as modern scientists have envisioned a socialist society where man can freely develop his talents and reasoning; where he can cultivate his feelings and grasp the richness and beauty of the world. Socialism has always been a concept of broader freedom for man. Marx saw future society as a realization of the humanist ideas of the past, as real communism, which frees man. Unless socialism brings to life the ideas from which it was born, it cannot bring to life Marx's program. Marxism is a program of human freedom, and if it is not this, it is not Marxism.

The guarantee of the humanist future of socialism lies only in the people themselves, in their actions. Unlike past centuries, when man was dragged through history as a sacrifice to his own needs, when he was a passive thing in the hands of blind social forces, constantly plagued by war, hunger, and oppression, the twentieth century offers man a chance to direct history. Only in our century have people realized that it is possible to change the world. If they go about it with full consciousness, they will not go against their own interests, will not transform themselves into a society of mechanized robots and prefabricated automatons, but will strive for the human content of future society. The actions of the people today, their knowledge that socialism does not exist without humanism, are of the utmost importance. Socialism is concerned not only with the development of productive forces and technology, but also with the content of social relationships, the problems of people and the character of man. Increased technology without a change in human relations can bring only the dark future of George Orwell's 1984, not socialism. The inhuman technocracy of Orwell's pessimistic utopia represents a world that has lost its humanist tradition. Socialism cannot relinquish this tradition without giving up the rationale of its existence and its roots. The people themselves are responsible for socialist humanism, and nobody can take responsibility away from them—not a strong personality, or weapons, or institutions, or technical perfection. The people alone, in their actions, must answer for the socialist content of humanism.

The Genius
and the Apparatus

[1968]

Master Chuang once dreamt that he was a butterfly, fluttering hither and thither. The butterfly felt like a butterfly, and lacked for nothing—it did not know that it was Chuang! Suddenly Chuang awoke and was amazed—he is Chuang! And he does not know if Chuang dreamt that he was a butterfly or if the butterfly is now dreaming that it is Chuang. Chuang or butterfly—surely there must be some difference! And that is what is called the mutability of phenomena.

—CHUANG-TZU, old Chinese philosopher

The Truth of Paradox

If Marx came to life and wished to define himself in relation to the image of Marx that has been built up since his death, he would find himself in the same situation as Chuang. Like the Chinese philosopher 2,000 years ago, Marx, too, would master the problem of the truth of paradox. He would do so through the antinomies and paradoxes of reality, for his genius is the highly developed, clear and precise consciousness of the self in the world and the world in the self; it is the transparent reflection of contemporary society in the consciousness of the individual. The more universal a genius is, the more he unites within himself scientific truth, the message of freedom and, unfortunately, the source for the cult of personality.

Marx the scholar is the Copernicus of social sciences; he brought about a transformation of the sciences dealing with man similar to that which marked the move from astrology to astronomy. In speaking of Marx as the Copernicus of social sciences, we are not implying that the founder of modern astronomy was infallible. It was Galileo who discovered that the orbit of planets around the sun is elliptical and not circular, as Copernicus himself believed. Similarly, modern social science reinterprets the functioning of man in the modern world but Marx's anthropocentric standpoint still holds true.

Marx was not, is not and will never be the discoverer and theoretician of totalitarian dictatorship that he appears today, when the original meaning of his work—true humanism—has been given a thoroughly Byzantine and Asian twist. Marx strove for a wider humanism than that of the bourgeois democracies that he knew and for wider civil rights, not for the setting up of the dictatorship of one class and one political party. What is today thought to be the Marxist theory of the state and Marxist social science is simply an ideological forgery, a false, modern conception as wrong as the idea that the orbits of heavenly bodies are circular.

To understand Marx truly, we must be aware how much he was conditioned by his time, determine his place in the development of theory, and not confuse his thought with the later interpretations by Lenin, Stalin and Mao. A true picture of Marx depends on an awareness of his historicity, while the ideological conceptions of "Marxism," "Marxism-Leninism" or "Maoism" are functional ideological tools used by apparatuses to manipulate the masses, not objective, truthful and historically valid interpretations. Just as it was necessary to separate Stalin from Lenin, so Lenin must be separated from Marx, not in order to oppose one against the other but so that both may be understood as real historical personalities.

If we approach the writings of Marx and Lenin in this historical, truthful and objective manner, then we must distinguish Marx's great thought about the liberating role of the working class in modern history from Lenin's specifically Russian thought about the leading role of the Communist party. Broadly speaking, Marx defended the leading role of the *working class*, he defended its historical mission and workers' activity as such, but he never imagined that this class itself might be dominated by a political party—and especially by the apparatus of this party. According to him, the dictatorship of the proletariat was to be the *temporary* rule of the *majority* over the minority, not the permanent terror of a minority against the people.

Marx relies on man, on the working class, on the people as the motive force of history, not on the manipulation of people. For him, man is the subject of the historical process, not an object to be manipulated by apparatuses. Lenin's concept of the Bolshevik party is fundamentally different. This is due to the basic realities of Czarist Russia—an ocean of illiteracy with a numerically weak working class. However, that does not make any less valid the criticism of Lenin's conception that was made by Plekhanov, by Rosa Luxemburg and by Trotsky.

Putting Leninism into effect in Russia led to the political triumph of the working class, to a victorious revolution and to the founding of a socialist state. Putting the same pattern into effect in Czechoslovakia, where the literate working class was already the strongest political force at the time the Communist party came into being and where it represented the majority of the population even at the very beginning of the building of socialism, has led to clear failure. It was, and is, just as inappropriate that the party should dominate the working class as that the party apparatus should dominate the state. And it is so not because we are against Marx or Lenin, but precisely because we are for Marx and for an understanding of the historical context in which Lenin specifically adapted Marx's heritage to Russia—not to Europe.

If we think of Marx the social scientist historically, bearing in mind the time in which he lived, the question of the timeless truth of his individual statements and opinions does not arise and we can appreciate the real worth of Marx's valid and still applicable methodology; moreover, we can turn it against his apparent disciples—the ideologists. To see how right this approach is, one has only to notice how violently the very people who claim to be Marxists hate the ruthless search for truth which is their master's methodology. The power apparatus has won all along the line against the real Marx, but in this it has only paradoxically confirmed the genius' paradoxical truth that institutions are stronger than people—a truth the genius had already arrived at in an essay he wrote at high school, whereas it took the apparatus a whole century to get there.

Because of its mass diffusion, the false image of Marx, as forged by ideologists of all shades in order to justify totalitarian dictatorship, cannot be corrected all at once. At the moment it is enough to say that the present process of democratization is being hampered not by Marx but by much more concrete individuals with much smaller intellectual capacities. We can hope that we shall defeat them, because reason alone can overcome power permanently.

The ideological caricature of Marx can perhaps be adequately conveyed by the absurdly surrealistic metaphor of one sociologist, for whom Marx, perverted and deformed in the consciousness of society, is a monster with two heads which are trying to shout each other down, one with Soviet and one with Chinese slogans. By contrast, the faithful, historical picture of the real Marx shows the scholar, the European, the democrat, the socialist, the tribune of the people, the humanist, the revolutionary, the internationalist, the giant personality and the messenger of freedom. This true picture of the man Marx really was has been transformed by the apparatuses of the movement and by history itself into an absolute labyrinth of contradictions.

The Message of Freedom

Marx was a social scientist of genius. But scientific knowledge continues to develop. Insofar as this means that the frontiers of knowledge are constantly expanding, Marx's scholarship is being outstripped by the evolution of the social science that he himself founded. In discovering a valid methodology of social science, Marx discovered a weapon against himself as a fetish-idol, against ideological authority and against the perversion of his own message of freedom.

Marx was an earnest European, with deep roots in the European culture based on antiquity, Christianity, the Renaissance and the Enlightenment. But his teaching was taken over in Eastern Europe and in Asia, where there was not only no Enlightenment but also no Renaissance. The core of Marx's discoveries—his criticism—had to be transformed into a bigoted orthodox faith in the unity of church and state, which took the shape of a monopoly of power, irreconcilable with the European cultural tradition, with criticism and with science.

Marx was one of the greatest democrats in history. He stood for human and civil rights as the basis of political life. But the rise of the giant bureaucratic apparatuses of the modern state, of industrial societies and of political machines, as well as the practical impossibility of following democratic procedures in Czarist Russia and then in a land of semiliteracy, have obstructed the development of those features of democracy which Marx took for granted, convinced as he was that "one form of freedom depends upon another. . . . Whenever a specific freedom is questioned, freedom itself becomes questionable."

Marx was a socialist; he strove to change production relations in order to emancipate the working class, humanity and man as an individual. But the narrow interpretation of his program in purely economic terms, as a program of future prosperity, has led to the technocratic effort to create a consumer society. The *means* to the emancipation of mankind have become an end, contrary to Marx's original intentions; for him, economic demands were only a means of liberating man, and not an end in themselves.

Marx was a tribune of the workers' movement in which he saw a guarantee that mankind would be liberated. But eventually organizations, apparatuses and even state apparatuses acquired power over the movement itself and stifled every spontaneous expression of the workers' will as treason against Marx. The greatest treason against Marx, however, is the very existence of these power apparatuses dominating the political movement of the working class.

Marx was a humanist, for whom the meaning of human life lay in creation, in the development of man as a many-sided personality, in people's participation in the historical process and in the growth of human freedom. But in the apparatus version of Marxism, these original aims, through which Marx hoped to achieve a revolutionary transformation, have been completely subordinated to the functional conception of man as a mere object to be manipulated. In the vocabulary of the apparatus, his central postulate, the freedom of man, has become a reactionary slogan; this is the most brutal castration that Marx has had to suffer.

Marx was a revolutionary fully aware of his goal. Being a radical humanist in the middle of the nineteenth century meant trying to bring about revolutionary change in the political and economic structure of society. But the transformation of the industrial countries of Europe that was brought about by the organized strength of the workers' movement set in motion processes which changed the social position of the working class, its opinions, its political goals and even the very nature of the revolution. The original conception that the proletarian revolution is a means of winning power is being changed by the radical transformation of science and technology; this is the true revolution, which is bringing mankind and the working class much closer to freedom than any fighting on the barricades.

Marx was an internationalist, for whom national frontiers were barriers to understanding between nations and between the working classes. But the doctrine of socialism in one country, which is incompatible with Marx's appeal to the workers of the world, has created a nationalistic pattern of cooperation between unequal nations. The ploughed-up stretches of land and the barbed wire between European countries are the most flagrant violation of the idea of internationalism. It is *against this idea* that the armed units stand on guard along the frontiers of socialist countries.

Marx was a great and many-sided personality, but he became the refuge of nonentities who knew, and still know, that they cannot hope to turn the zeros that they are into a positive number except by hiding behind his great figure. We need only compare the personality of Marx with that of today's leaders to become convinced that history has a sense of comedy as cruel as it is malicious.

Marx was a messenger of the freedom of man. That is why he attracted the hatred of apparatuses of all colors. And inasmuch as progress is the growth of human freedom, the living Marx will go on attracting their hatred. Just as the embalmed corpse of the ideology associated with his name will go on and on being exhumed in the solemn discourses of the official spokesmen of the apparatuses, who shower their decorations upon the dead genius only because he does not have the strength to throw the medals back in their faces in the name of the same working class which they would like to use as their vindication before the judgment of history.

The Lie of Salvation

The ideological conception of Marx is a perversion of the real Marx, which is being used to justify the domination of apparatuses over the workers' movement. Marx is at the same time turned into a myth, an irrational authority, into the guarantor of the faith in the messianic role of the working class in modern history, into the focal point of the prophetically foretold workings of the laws of history. But Marx is not a savior.

As the social function of his teaching has changed, Marx has been made a prophet, a visionary and a messiah; this was the outcome of the historical process in which, after his death, Marx's various scientific observations became norms of behavior to be regarded as absolutely valid for the whole labor movement. Thus the scientific analysis of capitalism gradually grew into a stereotype of ideological formulae; for quite a long time these did reflect the reality of capitalism, but nevertheless they lost their scientific character. Marx is not an earthly messiah.

As the discrepancies grew between Marx's analysis—perfectly accurate as regards the capitalism of his own time—and the reality at the turn of the century, and then in the period between the wars, so the giant of critical thought had to be smothered in thicker and thicker clouds of the incense of faith and turned into the impotent dummy of May Day parades. The gap between dogma and reality can be bridged only by faith—by faith in a leader, in the secular god of a mass movement, or by faith in an institution, in the secular church, which guarantees salvation to man. But Marx cannot be the object of faith; he is not a secular god.

As soon as the lie of salvation, that is, faith in the revolutionary, liberating mission of the Communist party, was substituted as a principle for the discipline of truth, the problem of faith and of the decline of faith emerged as the central issue. There came the break with the intellectuals who were unwilling to lay down their own intellect on the altar of the party, of the nation or of the movement. The famous statement "Believe the party, comrades," [1] and the endless discussions on whether the party is always right revealed the total bankruptcy of critical thought, which was all the more absurd for having been brought about in the name of Marx.

At the same time, the absurd statement about the party's being the guarantor of truth and the focus of faith reflects the deep crisis in the consciousness of the left-wing intellectuals of the 1950s. It reflects the tragic confusion in thought and in practice which accompanied not only the trials but also the establishment,

---

[1] Translator's note: After the executions that followed the Slansky trial, Czechoslovak President and party boss Klement Gottwald said in a speech that many comrades were asking, if so many party leaders had been traitors, whom were they to believe, and he answered, "Believe the party, comrades."

in the heart of Europe, of a measure of barbarity such as Czechs and Slovaks had previously experienced only at the hands of foreign invaders but never at the hands of representatives of their own nations. To this day, textbooks quote, as a warning example to schoolchildren of the inhumanity of a system based on slavery, the killing, 2,000 years ago, of the woman mathematician Hypatia by the mob of Alexandria, whom history holds fully responsible for the murder. Yet the present apparatuses are just as fully responsible for an act which is a unique performance in modern world history—the execution of a woman, Milada Horakova, for her political activity in time of peace.

Faith in the party was a defense against the appalling absurdities of life, which appeared totally incomprehensible and incompatible with the humanist goal that the ideology proclaimed in words and destroyed in practice. The psychological mechanisms, both individual and collective, of faith and despair, frustration and salvation explained, in a situation in which critical thought had totally ceased to function, attitudes toward the trials, toward the USSR or toward Stalin. Once the premises according to which the discipline of truth about reality is subordinated to party discipline and to faith in salvation through the party, were accepted, all that remained was to believe—to believe even beyond the grave, like those imprisoned Communists who died with Stalin's name on their lips.

The problem of faith—in the trials, in the party and in Stalin— also reflected the central issue, that is, the conviction that one has to accept guilt in order to save the meaning of one's former commitment to the cause of socialism, the meaning of the fight against fascism, the meaning of the building of socialism. The greater the doubts that arose, the higher did the flame of faith have to rise, the showier did the *auto da fé* have to be. And the readier was the average man to accept the stereotyped resolution of his doubts, presenting them *before his own conscience* as being inconsequential, insignificant in comparison with the cheering crowds, with the building of new plants and with the undoubtedly noble aim of helping the people, which was constantly put forward by the ideology as a reality, though in practice it did not exist.

Neither Marx nor the working class accepts the ghastly game of pinning medals on the breasts of corpses in the name of their murderers. Neither Marx nor the working class, nor indeed history, recognizes the rehabilitation of corpses, for, unlike the apologists for the apparatuses, they know very well what justice is. The working class, as Marx's heir, has a clean slate; it did not murder and persecute freedom, so it does not need the farce of the sinister ceremonies in which decorations are solemnly returned to corpses which accepted their appalling sacrifice as a rightful service to the same apparatuses which executed them and to which they had belonged. The working class, like the intellectuals, looks with horror upon this senseless performance, which is meant to exculpate the apparatus in the eyes of history; it can only see it as a provocation by the apparatus against common sense.

The baser the goals that are aimed at, the nobler must be the ideology that is used to justify them; for people do not normally have the courage to do evil, to hurt others or to spread suffering, unless the institutions of salvation, the church or the party, offer them sedatives to calm their conscience. Man cannot save himself through faith in a leader, in an ideology or an institution, he cannot, through his emotions, win heaven, or reason, or happiness, which is a secular term for salvation. But he can understand himself as a free, active, responsible being, with his own reason and feelings: then he will not be deaf to the true heritage of Marx, the genius whose last will and testament, translated into the language of today, might sound something like this:

YES	*NO*
to INTERNATIONALISM	to NATIONALISM
EUROPE	ASIA
SOVEREIGNTY	NEOCOLONIALISM
SOCIALISM	STATE CAPITALISM

DIRECT DEMOCRACY	DICTATORSHIP
DECENTRALIZATION	MONOPOLY OF POWER
CULTURE	APPARATUSES
HUMANISM	MANIPULATION
CRITICAL ATTITUDES	AUTHORITIES
THE PEOPLE	THE MASSES
THE INDIVIDUAL	THE ÉLITE
FREEDOM	ANARCHY

YES TO AN OPEN SOCIETY. NO TO TOTALITARIAN MECHANISMS. PEOPLE OF THE WORLD, UNITE AGAINST THE RATS OF THE WORLD. MARX IS DEAD. LONG LIVE MARX.

Editorial Remark

All essays in this book were written as public addresses, lectures, and discussions, and were given publicly—during the full flowering of the Stalinist regime in Czechoslovakia. With the exception of insignificant fragments, the censorship managed to stop publication, four times in some cases, so that the essays could be published only after the abolition of censorship in June 1968. All essays are translated by Jarmila Veltrusky from the Czech text without changes. They were selected so that the reader can understand the gradual radicalization of criticism and the variety of topics to which critical thought was applied.

The Art of Philosophy, 1956

Contribution to a philosophical discussion held in The Institute of Philosophy, Czechoslovak Academy of Science, in 1956 and printed partly in *Literární noviny*, Nos. 16 and 54, 1956, and in *Věda a Život*, 1964, No. 1. The whole essay was confiscated for the second time in Fall 1963 in a Slovak journal *Kulturny Zivot* and for the third time in 1967, with the whole book of essays, called *Human Face of Culture*.

Man and Poetry, 1963

Contribution to the discussion at the Conference on the Theory of Literature, organized by Czechoslovak Academy of Science, Liblice, 1963, published in *Ceská literatura*, No. 2, 1964.

Dramatic Models of Man, 1964

Paper read at a conference on Shakespeare, in the Theatre on the Balustrade, Divadlo na Zábradlí, Spring 1965, confiscated in the journal *Divadlo*.

Anthropological Conditions of Modern Culture, 1964

Paper read at the Conference on Education through Art, organized by the Socialist Academy, Spring 1964, confiscated as mimeographed manuscript.

Theory of Alienation, 1966

Lecture from the cycle "Philosophical Anthropology," given at the Faculty of Philosophy, Charles University, in Prague, November 1966. The whole course was banned by the Dean, before it was finished.

The Meaning of Marxism, 1966

Lecture from the cycle "Philosophical Anthropology," given at the Faculty of Philosophy, Charles University, in Prague, November 1966, published in *Student,* 1968.

The Sources of Socialist Humanism, 1963

Paper read at a conference "Man Today", Dubrovnik, Yugoslavia, 1963.

The Genius and the Apparatus, 1968

Lecture given May 3, 1968, at the Faculty of Philosophy, Charles University, Prague, to commemorate the fifteenth anniversary of Karl Marx. Published in *Student,* 1968.